YOUR ONE-STOP GUIDE TO THE SACRAMENTS

Your One-Stop Guide to the Sacraments

MSGR. DALE FUSHEK AND BILL DODDS

CHARIS

SERVANT PUBLICATIONS
ANN ARBOR, MICHIGAN

Charis Books is an imprint of Servant Publications especially designed to serve Roman Catholics.

Servant Publications—Mission Statement

We are dedicated to publishing books that spread the gospel of Jesus Christ, help Christians to live in accordance with that gospel, promote renewal in the church, and bear witness to Christian unity.

Scripture verses are taken from the Revised Standard Version of the Bible, copyrighted 1946, 1952, 1971 by the Division of Christian Education of the National Council of Churches of Christ in the USA. Used by permission. Excerpts from the English translation of the Catechism of the Catholic Church for use in the United States of America Copyright 1994, United States Catholic Conference, Inc.-Libreria Editrice Vaticana. Used with permission.

Servant Publications
P.O. Box 8617
Ann Arbor, MI 48107
www.servantpub.com

Cover design: Dave Hile Illustration and Design, Ann Arbor, Mich.

03 04 05 06 10 9 8 7 6 5 4 3 2 1

Printed in the United States of America
ISBN 1-56955-338-6

Library of Congress Cataloging-in-Publication Data

Fushek, Dale.
  Your one-stop guide to the sacraments / Dale Fushek and Bill Dodds.
      p. cm.
Includes index.
  ISBN 1-56955-338-6 (alk. paper)
  1. Sacraments–Catholic Church. 2. Catholic Church–Doctrines. I.
Dodds, Bill. II. Title.
  BX2200.F87 2003
  234'.16–dc21

                                                                        2003001574

Dedication

For my Catholic brothers Phil Baniewicz and Tom Booth,
who helped start and grow Life Teen.
—D.F.
For my cousin Fr. John W. Clarke.
—B.D.

Contents

ONE

God's Giving You a Sign

Sometimes life is confusing. Sometimes you just aren't sure what to do or how to do it. Sometimes you pray—fervently, desperately—"Dear God, just give me a sign! Give me a clue. Give me a hint.

"No need to actually point," you could add. "Just sort of nod. Just ... shoot me a little wink. Yeah, a wink."

A wink is a good sign, one that can mean:

- "Hey, you're looking good."
- "That's terrific. Thatta girl!" or "There ya go!"
- "You're in on the joke."

But God isn't known for his winking. You can scour Scripture and pore over the writings of the fathers of the Church, and you aren't going to find Isaiah or Paul or Augustine talking about winking. Same with the documents of Vatican II and the *Catechism of the Catholic Church.* God *could* shoot you a wink, of course, and not just because, being all-powerful, he can do anything. Rather, when you suggest, ask, demand (whisper, sing, shout), "Just give me a sign!" God could wink to tell you, "Already did. Already am."

God could wink because, created in his image, you *are* looking good. You *are* terrific. He *does* want you to succeed. So what's the joke? What's the inside scoop here?

Our all-loving Creator has given you—given us—seven signs: the sacraments. And they're infinitely better than any pointing, nodding, or winking. They're infinitely more than any clue or hint. They don't just give the answer; they *are* the answer.

It's Not Quite Greek to Us

They are the answer? What does that mean? Say, for instance, you're at the checkout stand and the clerk looks up from the scanner and asks, "Paper or plastic?" You, having been baptized, immediately respond ...

No, we need to think a little larger here. And we need to think a little smaller. Larger because this has to do with, well, the cosmos and beyond, the mind of God. And smaller because this has to do with what goes on inside you: your mind, your heart, your soul.

In the early Church—after Jesus' death, resurrection, and ascension—Christ's followers had a word for this God-You connection and what goes on there. That's where we get our English word *sacrament*. But if a concept is tossed around for a couple of thousand years, then, not surprisingly, it can lose some of its original meaning.

When we hear *sacrament,* most likely we think of baptism, Eucharist, confirmation, holy orders, marriage, reconciliation, and anointing of the sick (or of as many of those seven as we can rattle off the top of our heads). Our *sacrament* comes from the Latin *sacramentum,* meaning a sacred pledge. The

Latin is a translation of the Greek, which was used in the Church in those early centuries. So what we have is a translation of a translation, which can be a bit like a photocopy of a photocopy. Going back to the original can help us see what we're actually looking at now.

Sacramentum was one way the Greek word *musterion* was translated. The other way was *mysterium. Sacramentum* came to emphasize the visible sign of the hidden reality of salvation indicated by the term *mysterium.*

It came to do what that did what?

Here's a simple comparison from our own time: a bumper sticker that reads "I" and "my dog" with a Valentine's heart between them. The symbol of a heart—it certainly isn't an accurate drawing of a real human heart—stands for love. In this case it's a concrete sign of an abstract reality.

The Latin *mysterium* aspect of the Greek *musterion* is that fact that Christ himself was—and is—the mystery of salvation. Talk about cosmic! The sacraments are really part of the mystery that reveals God's love for each of us. And talk about personal! Way back then and right now, the sacraments are always about God's love for each and every human being. They're about his love for you.

They're also always about his love for his Church, because the seven sacraments are the signs and instruments by which the Holy Spirit spreads the grace of Christ (the Head of the Church) throughout it (his mystical body, and that includes all who have been baptized). So the Church both has and gives the invisible grace it "signifies." In this analogical sense, the Church is called a sacrament, too. It's a sign.

The bishops at Vatican II put it this way: "The Church is in

Christ like a sacrament or sign and instrument both of a very closely knit union with God and of the unity of the whole human race" ("Dogmatic Constitution on the Church," 1, 1). It's the "sacrament" of salvation.

Yahweh Tipped His Hand; Jesus Spilled the Beans

But what was—is—"the mystery of Jesus"?

In the ordinary language of those earlier times, *musterion* or *mysterion* had to do with the secret religious rites of cults. When it's used in the Gospels (Mk 13:11; 14:11; and Lk 8:10), it refers to the mystery of the kingdom, which is revealed explicitly to the disciples but to others only in parables. The evangelists don't define it specifically. Scripture scholars point out it can only be defined from the general context of the Gospels. They say most interpreters believe that it is the present reality of the kingdom in the person of Jesus, which is recognized only by revelation. The basic sense of "mystery" in the New Testament is an object of divine revelation.

St. Paul says the wisdom of God is a mystery (1 Cor 2:7). The Almighty's plan of salvation is the only true wisdom, and we can't figure it out by rational speculation or deduction. It's beyond Sherlock Holmes, Nancy Drew, Columbo—or us.

But our generous God, to quote Ephesians 1:9, "has made known to us the mystery of his will." He realizes we can't get it on our own. So he tells us. He reveals himself over time to one particular group of people, and then he comes himself and says what's what.

Yahweh tips his hand to the chosen people. That's what's happening in the Old Testament.

Jesus is born a human being and lives among us. That's at the core of the Gospels. His disciples believe his message—his mystery—and then start to tell others. That's the Acts of the Apostles and the rest of the New Testament. That, in a nutshell, is the role of the Church on earth.

So what's the plan? What's *his* plan? To bring all things under one head in Christ. Unknown in ancient times, the Spirit revealed it to the Old Testament prophets and then to the apostles. When they "got it"—or, more accurately, got glimpses or flashes of it—that was the Spirit's doing.

With the coming of Christ, the mystery was no longer a secret. In non-biblical terms, Jesus spilled all the beans. But it remains, for us, a mystery. Even as we can know it, we can't really "get it." Our (God-given) faith gives us the ability to believe while we're here on earth. But that's not the same as the rock-solid satisfaction of the "Ah ha!" that comes from properly sleuthing out Professor Plum in the library with the lead pipe.

After Christ's ascension, not only was the mystery no longer a secret, the apostles' task—obligation, prime directive—was to go out and tell the world. By that telling they would draw others to God. Jesus said they were to do that by "baptizing them in the name of the Father and of the Son and of the Holy Spirit" (Mt 28:19).

A *musterion*, then, in the early Church also meant a profound spiritual truth. A sacrament was—and is—a profound spiritual truth. The Eastern Church still refers to the sacraments as the "seven mysteries."

While we've come to use a form of the word *sacramentum*, we still use "mystery" in that sense, too. For example, the twenty events we meditate on in the rosary, and the spiritual truths each reveals, are known as the joyful, sorrowful, glorious, and luminous mysteries. And at every Mass, immediately following the consecration, the celebrant invites the congregation, "Let us proclaim the mystery of faith." We answer, "Christ has died, Christ is risen, Christ will come again."

We know it. It's not a secret. We proclaim it in a single sentence, and we believe it even as we don't fully understand it (and work at believing it when our faith is shaky).

The seven sacraments—those seven mysteries—are God's plan for his Church and for all people. They're his plan for you.

So Simple a Seven-Year-Old Could ...

We're lucky. We have no trouble defining what a sacrament is because we've been handed a cracker-jack definition. If you were in a Catholic grade school or CCD—religious education—class in the forties, fifties, or early sixties, you probably memorized it. Given a bit of a push, a mental jump-start, you could probably recite it still.

"A sacrament is an outward sign ... "—feel those old wheels turning?—"instituted by Christ to give grace."

Why was that the definition? As a second-grader, it was because "Sister said." Case closed. Even as a lay adult in that era, not infrequently it was because "it's what the catechism says." Case closed.

But why did the catechism say that? And was the standard religious education book used in the United States at that time—known as the Baltimore Catechism—correct?

Jesus never told his apostles, "Look, I'm going to start seven sacraments. They'll give you grace. With me so far? OK, here's the deal with each one. Listen up."

No, through what he said and what he did, he revealed to the apostles—to the Church, to us—everything we have to know about God's will. But we humans needed some time—still need some time—to come to understand what that divine revelation is. This is known as the development of doctrine. Over centuries some of the brightest minds and holiest people, led by the Spirit, have increased our understanding of what Christ gave us.

Now looking back almost two thousand years, it's possible to trace the development of what we know about the sacraments and to pinpoint some people—saints and theologians and saints who were theologians—and some Church councils that helped us get where we are today. (Go to "Who's Who and What's What," p. 23) When the Church puts together a book to help us learn about the sacraments (or about any other doctrine, any other truth revealed to us by Christ), it uses those teachings. That's what the Catechism of the Catholic Church offers.

First published in 1994, it explains that the Church, led by the Spirit, who guides it into all truth, "has gradually recognized this treasure received from Christ and, as the faithful steward of God's mysteries, has determined its 'dispensation' [meaning how this "treasure" is administered]. Thus the Church has discerned over the centuries that among liturgical celebrations there are seven that are, in the strictest sense of the term, sacraments instituted by the Lord" (CCC 1117).

So even though the Bible doesn't use our word *sacrament,* the reality that the Church teaches now is firmly grounded in both Scripture and Tradition. (Tradition is the living transmission of the message of the gospel in the Church.) Both have their common source in Jesus. *(Go to "And the Bible Says ... "* p. 26.)

What do they, what does the Church, teach about the sacraments?

What Jesus said and did during his "hidden" life and public ministry was "salvific"—that is, saving. His words and actions anticipated the power of the Paschal-Easter mystery: the redemption of us all. They announced and they prepared what he was going to give the Church (us!) when "all was accomplished." The mysteries—there's that word again—of Christ's life remain the foundation of what he would later dispense in the sacraments, through the ministers of his Church.

The *Catechism* points out that those seven sacraments are

- powers that come forth from the body of Christ, which is ever-living and life-giving
- actions of the Holy Spirit at work in his body, the Church
- "the masterworks of God" in the new and everlasting covenant (A covenant is a contract, a deal. The Old Testament can be called the old covenant; the New Testament is the new covenant.) (CCC 1116)

None of Us Really "Get It"

In the middle of all this theology, history, and etymology (word business), it's time to pause for a moment and clearly say that this book isn't written so that you can do well on a theology, history, or etymology exam. The purpose is to help you better receive the sacraments by better understanding them. But you—we, anyone on earth—never will understand them fully. The grace they offer centers on faith, not understanding. They have to do with God's wisdom, not our knowledge.

Even so, the more we learn about this mystery, the more we can marvel at God's gift in the sacraments (even as we recognize how little we know about it). If anything, increasing our knowledge increases our humility so that we become more like little children: simple (to put it bluntly) but sincere.

At the same time, our limitations don't relieve us of the obligation to work toward better understanding the sacraments. Not so that we'll be considered smart but so that, to say it again, we can take better advantage of the gift.

The point here is that, even as you read about each sacrament, don't be discouraged if you don't "get it." Ultimately, it's the Holy Spirit who can help you better understand what the Holy Spirit offers. And his giving doesn't rely on your knowledge. We don't "deserve" the sacraments because we're so smart or because we're so good.

We'll never be that smart, never be that good.

Signs by and for the Church

We need to talk a little bit more about the fundamental relationship between the Church and the sacraments. The sacraments are "of the Church," meaning both by it and for it. They're "by it" because the Church is the sacrament—the sign—of Christ's action in it through the mission of the Holy Spirit. At the same time, they're "for it," to quote the *Catechism*, "in the sense that 'the sacraments make the Church,' since they manifest and communicate to men, above all in the Eucharist, the mystery of communion with the God who is love, One in three persons" (CCC 1118).

Expanding on the definition memorized by seven-year-olds a generation or two ago, the *Catechism* notes that the sacraments

a. are efficacious signs of grace
b. were instituted by Christ
c. are entrusted to the Church
d. are a means by which life is dispensed to us

And the visible rites by which the sacraments are celebrated (the "matter" and "form," to use the theological terms—what's used, done, and said)

e. signify and make present the graces proper to each sacrament
f. bear fruit in those who receive them with the required dispositions

Let's back up to a, b, and c. "Instituted by Christ" (he began them) and "entrusted to the Church" (it dispenses them) aren't so hard to understand. But "efficacious"? What's an "efficacious sign"? (And grace? *Go to "Q & A: What's the Deal With Grace, and Why Would I Want It?"* p. 28.)

Everywhere a Sign

We humans love signs and use signs because signs work, sometimes instantly. They're such a part of our ordinary life, we seldom think about them even as we rely on them. Whether a gesture, word, or symbol, a sign says something that's easily recognized and understood by most of the people for whom it's intended.

In everyday language, a "sign" can be that playful wink. It can be a piece of metal that says STOP. In some cases a sign works worldwide. The icon of the martini glass on the side of a box tells a customer in Kobe, Japan, or Nairobi, Kenya, that the shipment from a company in Stockholm, Sweden, contains breakable items.

And not all signs are human-made. There are natural signs that we humans have figured out and continue to depend on. Where there's smoke there's ...? Of course, fire. Not always. There can be smoke without fire and fire without much smoke, but if we see, smell, or even suspect smoke in our home, we investigate. Smoke is an effective if not always accurate sign.

Those are all *effective* signs. None are *efficacious*. The wink doesn't make the person's words funny but only indicates he means them to be. A stop sign doesn't slam on a car's brakes but only commands the driver to halt. An icon on the outside of a box doesn't make its contents breakable but only warns that they are breakable. And smoke does not cause fire. ("How did you get the blaze out so quickly, Chief?" "Well, we were able to get rid of all the smoke.")

Efficacious Signs

Just as there are natural signs and human signs, there are supernatural signs. The seven sacraments—those divinely instituted signs—have always been efficacious, though it took the Church awhile to understand that, to develop that doctrine. The sacraments don't just say something or remind us of something; they *do* what they say and what they remind us of. "Celebrated worthily in faith, the sacraments confer the grace that they signify," to quote the *Catechism* (CCC 1127).

That's the case because Christ himself is at work in them—each time, every time, in the first century and in the twenty-first. He's the one acting "in order to communicate the grace that each sacrament signifies." Each sacrament produces what it intends. The intention is to give grace to the recipient.

The sacraments act *ex opere operato* (Latin for "by the very fact of the action being performed"). From the instant a sacrament is celebrated in accordance with the intention of the Church, the power of Jesus and the Holy Spirit acts in it and through it. And that happens "independently of the personal holiness of the minister" (CCC 1128). It happens whether the priest is a saint or not-so-saintly.

Does all this seem too good to be true? Do you suspect there has to be a catch? There's no fine print that changes the deal here, but the recipient does bear some responsibility. "The fruits of the sacraments also depend on the disposition of the one who receives them" (CCC 1128).

The grace is always there. We always have the free will to refuse it or to ignore it, to only nibble at it instead of feasting on it. God doesn't use the sacraments to make us holy whether we want to be holy or not. But each time we're offered the opportunity to receive a sacrament, we have the opportunity to experience Jesus.

A sacrament isn't like a manual where we "book learn" about Christ. It's where, it's how, we—you—can experience him. And that experience always happens within the community of the Church through its liturgies. The sacraments can't be celebrated independently of the Church, not because of some "rules" but because of their very nature, because of how Jesus gave them to us.

Again, from the *Catechism:* "It is the whole *community,* the Body of Christ united with its Head, that celebrates. 'Liturgical services are not private functions but are celebrations of the Church, which is the "sacrament of unity," namely, the holy people united and organized under the authority of the bishops'" (CCC 1140, quoting Vatican II, "Constitution on the Sacred Liturgy," 26).

That communal aspect is there even when the sacrament seems to be celebrated one-on-one, as in the sacrament of reconciliation or the anointing of the sick if only the priest and recipient are there. Always they are from Christ, through and in the Church, to us—to you.

Ultimately, the purpose of the sacraments is to change the individual and to change the world. Change the world? Yes, they have that kind of power, because in every celebration of a sacrament the Paschal mystery is celebrated. They are expressions of the death and resurrection of Christ that allow the individual and the community to really enter into both those events.

Choose Grace

Those seven signs, each distinct but all sharing that common "treasure," remain an incredible opportunity, a source of divine assistance that's unique because they were begun by Christ and delivered by the Holy Spirit. They are one-of-a-kind because they're efficacious. They give what they promise—always. And what they promise is beyond description, beyond superlatives, beyond anything we can ask or imagine. They allow us to share a sliver of—get a taste of, catch a glimmer of—what is to come, or more accurately, what can come for each of us because Jesus came, lived, and died on earth for each of us.

Because of Christ's redemption, just as we have the opportunity to "choose" heaven because we have free will, we have the privilege, time and again, to experience that sliver, that taste, that glimmer here on earth.

One of the true joys of being a Catholic is taking advantage of its "sacramentality," of the sacraments it administers, the sacraments it celebrates. And *celebrates* is the perfect word for what is *really* happening at these liturgies. (That's true no matter how we may feel at a particular Mass or other liturgy.

At a time when it's common to hear, "All religions are the same," or, "All Christian denominations are the same," the reality of the sacraments politely says, "No, that isn't so." The seven sacraments are one of the ways the Catholic Church is different. When asked, "Why be Catholic?" a brief answer can be, "Baptism, reconciliation, Eucharist, confirmation, holy orders, matrimony, and anointing of the sick."

In this book we're going to look at each of them. We'll talk about the "form" and "matter" that are used. And we'll examine what the Church teaches.

In the final chapter we'll focus on how to better take advantage of these gifts from God. We'll include how to do that if you're a practicing Catholic, a Catholic who's unable to receive them, or a Catholic who's been away from the Church for a time. We'll look at how to benefit from the sacraments even if you aren't a Catholic.

More than gifts from God, the sacraments are gifts *of* God, his gifts to us.

Who's Who and What's What

Tertullian (c. 160–c. 222): He's credited with a lot of "firsts": He's considered the first true theologian of the West (the Roman Church). He was the first Christian author to write mainly in Latin and the first to use the term *sacrament*. By it, generally, he meant many different aspects of God's plan to save us. Specifically, he used it to refer to baptism, Eucharist, and confirmation. He wrote of the flesh being "washed," "nourished," and "annointed."

St. Augustine (353–430): This great doctor of the Church used the principles of Greek philosophy when he taught that a sign is something that imprints a double image on the senses. The first is its distinctive image; the second is the further reality that pops into the mind of the one who sees it. For example, the Statue of Liberty is a metal sculpture of a woman holding a torch. Pop! It says, "The United States," or "Freedom."

Applying that principle, Augustine concluded that a sacred sign must lead one to a sacred or religious reality. Grace comes from this sacred sign because it is Christ himself who is at work.

St. Augustine wrote that any sacrament has two requirements: matter and form. The matter is what's seen and felt. The form—or formula—is the words that are spoken.

Each sacrament must also have a minister and a subject: one who gives the sign and one who receives it. Each of those has a basic requirement. The subject must be properly disposed, and the minister must intend to do what the Church does or wants done.

Peter Lombard (c. 1100–1160): For a brief time, Italian-born Peter Lombard was the bishop of Paris, but he's best known for writing *Book of Sentences,* also called simply the *Sentences.* It was *the* text for theological study until St. Thomas Aquinas' *Summa Theologiae* took the top spot. Lombard, like St. Augustine and others, emphasized that the worthiness (or, in some cases, unworthiness!) of the minister of a sacrament isn't a factor. That person's role is just that of a person who ministers. It's subordinate. The primary role always belongs to Christ.

St. Thomas Aquinas (1225–74): The great Dominican theologian said the sacraments are directly connected to the Incarnation—Jesus' being born a human—and the Paschal (or Easter) mystery. They aren't simply God's giving humans grace (although that should hardly be called "simply") but Jesus'—that is, God's—coming to earth and through his humanity touching human lives. At the same time, the sacraments are an intimate part of the Church, the mystical body of Christ. Through them come new life and healing. Members grow in grace, and the whole body is renewed.

Council of Trent (1545–63): This gathering of bishops authorized the Roman Catechism. It stated:

> But of the many definitions, each of them sufficiently appropriate, which may serve to explain the nature of a Sacrament, there is none more comprehensive, none more clearly written, perspicuous [clearly expressed and easy to understand], than the definition given by St. Augustine and adopted by the scholastic writers [of the late Middle Ages]. A sacrament, he says, is a sign of a sacred thing; or, as it has been expressed in other words of the same import: A sacrament is a visible sign of an invisible grace, instituted for our justification (II, Introduction).

Vatican Council II (1963–65): In their "Constitution on the Sacred Liturgy" the bishops explained:

> The purpose of the sacraments is to sanctify men, to build up the Body of Christ, and, finally, to give worship

25

to God. Because they are signs they also instruct. They not only presuppose faith, but by words and objects they also nourish, strengthen, and express it. That is why they are called "sacraments of faith." They do, indeed, confer grace, but, in addition, the very act of celebrating them most effectively disposes the faithful to receive this grace to their profit, to worship God duly, and to practice charity (59).

(Go to "The Sacraments and Vatican II," p. 27.)

Code of Canon Law (1983): The new Code of Canon Law—the revised version that replaced the 1917 edition—noted: "The sacraments of the New Testament, instituted by Christ the Lord and entrusted to the Church, as they are the actions of Christ and the Church, stand out as the signs and means by which the faith is expressed and strengthened, worship is rendered to God, and the sanctification of humankind is effected."

And the Bible Says ...

God has had some things to say about the sacraments, too. In fact, the sacraments are rooted in his Word:

Baptism: Matthew 28:19; Romans 6:3-11.
Reconciliation: Luke 15; John 20:21-23; 2 Corinthians 2:5-11.
Eucharist: Luke 22:19-20; 1 Corinthians 11:23-29.
Confirmation: Luke 24:49; Acts 8:14-17; Acts 19:1-6; 1 Corinthians 12:4-11.
Marriage: John 2:1-11; Matthew 9:15; Mark 10:11-12; Ephesians 5:21-33.

Holy orders: 2 Timothy 1:6; Titus 1:5-9.

Anointing of the sick: Mark 1:32-34; 6:13; James 5:14-15.

The Sacraments and Vatican II

When the bishops met at the Second Vatican Council (1962–65), they didn't "reform" or "update" the Catholic Church. They didn't "modernize" it, even as they considered its essential role in the modern world. Inspired and led by the Holy Spirit, they examined how it was at that point compared to how it had been at its beginning. They looked at how it could be restored.

They looked at how and why the Church did what it did in the mid-twentieth century. What methods, what actions in its rites and liturgies, had been added over the years that would be better altered or even eliminated? What did the twentieth-century Church—and beyond—want to teach and preach more boldly and more clearly, and how could it do that?

The result was that the same Spirit who blew through the upper room on Pentecost blew through the Church in our own era. The restorations the bishops set in motion in so many areas, including all seven sacraments and the Mass, didn't happen overnight. (And because the Church on earth remains a Spirit-led "work in progress," the task won't be complete until the end of time.)

Yet, truth be told, the outcome rattled more than a few people, both Catholic and non-Catholic. Many of the now senior and middle-age generations grew up in a Catholic atmosphere that hadn't altered much in some four hundred years—since the Council of Trent. They had understandably thought the Church would remain exactly as it had been in their own childhood. Just about any change would be startling, and the restorations, in some instances, seemed extremely radical.

They were "radical," of course, in the truest definition of that word. They returned the Church to its roots. At its roots it is, as we profess at every Sunday Mass, "apostolic." It contains and offers what Christ taught and gave his apostles.

Q & A: What's the Deal With Grace, and Why Would I Want It?

Why does God have to use the sacraments to give grace?
He doesn't. It was his choice, and he certainly isn't limited to giving grace only by means of the sacraments. He has no limits.

Then why did he give us the sacraments?
He loves us. As our Creator, he knows signs can help us understand a deeper reality: the outpouring of his grace.

What's grace?
It's the free and undeserved gift that God gives us so that we can respond to our vocation to become his adopted children. We were made to spend eternity with him. Grace leads us home.

There are three kinds of grace:

1. Sanctifying grace is God's sharing his divine life and friendship with us in a habitual gift. It's a stable and supernatural disposition that enables the soul to live with God and to act by his love.

---

2. Actual grace is God's giving us the help to conform our lives to his will.

3. Sacramental grace and special graces or charisms are gifts from the Holy Spirit to help us live our Christian vocation.

What are sacramentals?
They're sacred signs instituted by the Church that resemble the sacraments. They can be objects or actions—holy water or the sign of the cross, for example, both of which can remind a person of baptism. The Code of Canon Law explains: "Somewhat in imitation of the sacraments, sacramentals are sacred signs by which spiritual effects especially are signified and are obtained by the intercession of the Church" (*Codex Iuris Canonici* 1166).

Does the Church just make up how the sacraments are celebrated?
No, it can't do that. When the Church celebrates the sacraments, it's confessing—proclaiming, saying it believes—the faith received from the apostles. The Latin expression for this is *lex orandi, lex credendi:* The Church believes as it prays. The liturgy is a "constitutive element of the holy and living Tradition" (CCC 1124). It's basic, fundamental, part of the foundation.

That's why a sacramental rite can't be modified or manipulated at the will of the minister or the community. So, for example, a parish can't decide to replace the bread and wine at Mass with pretzels and beer because it's the weekend of Oktoberfest. "Even the supreme authority in the Church may not change the liturgy arbitrarily, but only in the obedience of faith and with religious respect for the mystery of the liturgy" (CCC 1125).

"Mystery!" Again.

TWO

Baptism: Your Ticket to Life

You need water to live. You use water to clean. Not surprisingly then, it's commonly assumed the water of baptism is meant to symbolize both. While it is and it does, that's not its only message.

The water of this first sacrament also represents death. It isn't that you're already alive and need water to stay that way. It isn't that you're doing all right and need it to get yourself spiffed up a bit. You're dead. You've drowned. Your body is still submerged.

Dead from what? Drowned in what? Still submerged in what? Sin. At the moment of your birth you enter a world flooded with sin and the terrible consequences that naturally flow from sin. No, it's not your fault as an infant. It's your inheritance.

Later, once you reach the age of reason and can determine right from wrong, you add to it. You choose wrong. You raise the water level. We all do.

Talk about depressing! Talk about pessimistic! Talk about reality.

Alone or even with the help of others, just as dead as we are, there's no reason to hope. The mess we find ourselves in and the mess we continue to contribute to is beyond anything we can fix. It's a dilemma we can't solve.

That's why the Word—Jesus—"became flesh and dwelt among us" (Jn 1:14). The symbolic water of this first sacrament is designed to bluntly, forcefully, crudely tell us: Through baptism, with baptism, in baptism, you who are already dead are brought to life through Christ, with Christ, in Christ.

New Life, New Lifestyle

In the early Church baptisms commonly took place at the Easter Vigil to reinforce the relationship between an individual's entering a new life and Jesus' own resurrection. In our own time, the rite—how the sacrament is celebrated—has returned to using submersion (rising from death) as well as pouring (which can seem to primarily indicate cleansing).

In the early Church, and now, too, that new life demands a new lifestyle. No longer dead *in* sin, we're called to be dead *to* sin. Being baptized means entering an Easter way of life, which is resurrection. That includes

- discipleship: A disciple is a student. We're to learn from Christ. (While *disciple* and *apostle* are sometimes used interchangeably, all the apostles, a word that means "messengers," were disciples, but not all Christ's disciples were apostles.)
- conversion: the ongoing process of turning toward God and turning away from sin
- surrendering to the life of Christ: dying to self and letting Christ live in us

Baptism in Scripture

In the liturgy of the Easter Vigil the Church points out how baptism was prefigured in the Old Testament in several places: the Spirit of God hovering over the waters at the time of creation, Noah's ark and the great flood, the journey of the Israelites through the Red Sea and the Jordan River, and the foretelling of divine cleansing in Ezekiel 36:25.

In the New Testament Jesus was baptized by his kinsman John—the Baptist (see Mt 3:13-17). John didn't "invent" what he did. There was a ritual of baptism before the time of Christ, though it wasn't a sacrament. There are indications it was practiced by a group of Hebrews—the sect of Qumran—before John's time. And John may have had a connection with that group.

Even as John baptized, he taught that what he was doing was not what the Messiah would do. And just as Jesus didn't need the sacrament of baptism, he didn't need the rite as it was performed by John either. Rather, Jesus voluntarily stepped forward to receive this baptism of repentance—which was intended for sinners—"to fulfill all righteousness" (Mt 3:15). That means he did perfectly whatever was just and designed to make just, because he was obedient to the will of God. His act of submission also demonstrated self-emptying (see Ti 2:7: "Show yourself in all respects a model of good works...."").

At Jesus' baptism in the Jordan River, the Spirit who had hovered over the waters of creation descended "as a prelude of the new creation" (CCC 1224). And it was the Father who revealed that Jesus is God's own "beloved Son."

In his Passover Jesus opened to all of us "the fountain of Baptism" (CCC 1225). He had already talked about his passion as a "baptism" with which he had to be baptized (Mk 10:38). The *Catechism* explains that "the blood and water that flowed from the pierced side of the crucified Jesus are types of Baptism and the Eucharist, the sacraments of new life" (CCC 1225; see Jn 19:34; 1 Jn 5:6-8).

It's from that point in history that it's possible for each of us to be "born of water and the Spirit" in order to enter the kingdom of God (see Jn 3:5). St. Ambrose (c.340-97) put it this way: "See where you are baptized, see where Baptism comes from, if not from the cross of Christ, from his death. There is the whole mystery: he died for you. In him you are redeemed, in him you are saved."

While the apostles, with the exception of John, were scared to death, or more accurately scared *of* death, at the time of Christ's passion, even after the Resurrection they remained timid and confused. It was on Pentecost that, on fire with the Spirit, they stepped out and stepped up. It was on Pentecost that they followed Christ's command and began baptizing.

The second chapter of the Acts of the Apostles tells us about that day. The astounded crowd asked what they had to do to get whatever it was the apostles had been given. Peter answered that they needed to repent and be baptized in Jesus' name for the forgiveness of their sins. While the sacrament is open to anyone who believes in Jesus, it's always seen as connected with faith.

In his Letter to the Romans Paul asks: "Do you not know that all of us who have been baptized into Christ Jesus were baptized into his death? We were buried therefore with him by baptism into death, so that as Christ was raised from the dead by the glory of the Father, we too might walk in newness of life" (6:3-4).

Paul also says that the baptized have "put on Christ" (Gal 3:27), and through the Holy Spirit, this sacrament is a bath that purifies, justifies, and sanctifies (see 1 Cor 6:11; 12:13).

The Rite of Christian Initiation of Adults

While there were "three thousand" people baptized on that first Pentecost (a huge round number that the author chose to mean "a lot"), the early Church soon developed a method and process for bringing people into the body that's still used today.

The Second Vatican Council restored the "catechumenate" for adults for the Latin Church. Those distinct steps are now the Rite of Christian Initiation of Adults (RCIA) or, as it's known in some parishes, the Order of Christian Initiation (OCI). The result is that how a person joining the Church reaches baptism more accurately reflects the process in apostolic times.

Catechumenate comes from the Greek for "instruction." In RCIA terms, "catechumens" are those who have never been baptized. "Candidates" are those who have been baptized in a Protestant church and are now coming into full communion with the Catholic Church. In some parishes candidates include baptized Catholics who have never received the sacraments of Eucharist and confirmation.

By the mid-twentieth century "taking instructions" had

become a few meetings with Father in the rectory parlor and a quiet, private ceremony in the back of the church. Not anymore. It could be argued that the couple-of-meetings method was easier for both the parish priest and the person seeking baptism. Vatican II's restoration didn't mean streamlining. If anything, the RCIA places more demands on both, and on the other parish members who are a part of this "journey" to baptism.

Now the process includes

- an initial period of inquiry, instruction, and evangelization. There are no secrets. There is no fine print. The Church wants those seeking—considering, wondering about, curious about—baptism to know the full story.
- the catechumenate, a period of at least a year of formal instruction and progressive formation in, and familiarity with, Christian life. It starts with a statement of purpose and includes the rite of election. That doesn't mean a vote is taken. The "elect" are the catechumens and candidates.
- immediate preparation, called a period of purification and enlightenment, from the beginning of Lent to reception of the sacraments of initiation—baptism, confirmation, Eucharist—during the Easter Vigil. This period is marked by scrutinies (judging the person's readiness for baptism), the formal recitation of the creed and the Lord's Prayer, the choice of a Christian name, and a final statement of intention.
- a "mystagogic" phase (from the Greek for, loosely translated, "leading a rookie"). The objective here is to gain

greater familiarity with Christian life in the Church through observance of the Easter season and through the catechumen's association with the community of the faithful and extended formation for about a year. In a sense, the mystagogic phase never ends for any Catholic, including those baptized as infants. We're each called to spend all our life reflecting on the importance of baptism, that incredible gateway leading to a particular and personal relationship with God.

The RCIA process is a little different for a candidate. Instruction and formation are provided as necessary, and conditional baptism is administered if there is reasonable doubt about the validity of the person's previous baptism.

In the rite of reception the candidate is invited to join the community of the Church in professing the Nicene Creed. He or she is asked to state: "I believe and profess all that the holy Catholic Church believes, teaches, and proclaims as revealed by God." The priest places his hand on the head of the person, says the formula of admission to full communion, confirms (if the bishop isn't there), gives a sign of peace, and administers Holy Communion during a eucharistic liturgy.

Baptizing Babies

Infant baptism isn't something new. There's explicit testimony describing it from the second century on, and it may have been a practice during the time of the apostles' preaching. The Acts of the Apostles (16:15, 33) and the First Letter to the

Corinthians (1:16) mention whole "households" who received baptism, and that well may have included their youngest members.

Why would an infant—one so innocent—be baptized? Why would he or she need to be baptized? Again, it's because we're born into a world steeped in sin, and we inherit original sin. *(Go to "Q & A: What's the Deal With Original Sin and With Godparents?" p. 47.)* "Children also have need of the new birth in Baptism to be freed from the power of darkness and brought into the realm of the freedom of the children of God," to which all of us are called (CCC 1250).

Infant baptism clearly demonstrates that we do nothing to deserve the grace of salvation. Just as a baby can't "earn" this gift from God, neither can any adult. Then, too, "the Church and the parents would deny a child the priceless grace of becoming a child of God were they not to confer Baptism shortly after birth" (CCC 1250).

One analogy that falls far short is that grace—that gift of God in us—is like the inoculations that protect an infant from the diseases to which all humans are susceptible. Any loving mom and dad want the optimal physical, mental, emotional, and spiritual health for their little one. In the early Church and now, Christian parents "recognize that this practice also accords with their role as nurturers of the life that God had entrusted to them" (CCC 1251).

For an infant to be baptized, at least one parent or a guardian has to give consent, and there has to be a realistic hope that the child will be raised in the Catholic faith. This sacrament isn't done for show. It isn't celebrated just to make Grandma happy.

The Code of Canon Law says that an infant in danger of death can be lawfully baptized even if his parents are opposed (Canons 865.1, 868.1-2).

Signs and Forms, Symbols and Words

As with all the sacraments, baptism uses signs and forms—symbols and words—that help us understand what is taking place.

The sign of the cross as the celebration begins marks the person with the imprint of Christ. It shows that he or she is going to belong to Christ, and it signifies the grace of the redemption Jesus won for all of us by his cross.

The proclaiming of the Word of God—the scriptural readings—enlightens those to be baptized and the congregation with the revealed truth. It elicits the response of faith, and that's inseparable from baptism. Baptism is called "the sacrament of faith" in a particular way because it's the sacramental entry into the life of faith.

Because this sacrament signifies liberation from sin and from its "instigator"—that is, Satan—one or more exorcisms are pronounced over the person. This doesn't mean he or she is possessed by the devil—as in some movie—but again, that each of us is born with original sin, lives in a world steeped in sin, and so leans toward sin.

The celebrant anoints the person with the oil of catechumens or lays hands on him, and the candidate explicitly renounces Satan. The baptismal water is consecrated by a prayer of "epiclesis"—a calling down of the Holy Spirit—either right then or previously at the Easter Vigil. The Church asks God that through his Son the power of the Spirit may be sent upon the water so that those who will be baptized in it may be "born of water and the Spirit" (Jn 3:5).

The essential rite has four signs: water, oil, light, and white clothing.

Water

In its most expressive way, baptism is performed by immersing the person in water three times. But from ancient times it has alternately been conferred by pouring water over the head three times.

In the Latin Church the minister says: "N. [that is, the person's Christian name], I baptize you in the name of the Father, and of the Son, and of the Holy Spirit." In Eastern liturgies the catechumen turns toward the East, and the priest prays: "The servant of God, N., is baptized in the name of the Father, and of the Son, and of the Holy Spirit." At the invocation of each Person of the Trinity, the priest immerses the person in the water, then raises him or her up.

(We have a reminder of this each time we enter our parish church. Dipping our fingers in the holy water font, putting a dab of water on our own forehead, and making the sign of the cross form a sacramental designed to call to mind that through the water of baptism and the sign of the cross, we entered the Church.)

Oil

The person is anointed with sacred chrism, perfumed oil that has been consecrated by the bishop. This signifies the gift of the Holy Spirit to the newly baptized. Now a Christian, she or he has been "anointed" by the Holy Spirit and incorporated in

Christ, who is anointed priest, prophet, and king.

In the Eastern Churches the post-baptismal anointing is the sacrament they call chrismation (and the one we in the Latin Church refer to as confirmation). In the Roman liturgy the post-baptismal anointing announces that second anointing that will be conferred later by the bishop. It will "confirm" and complete the baptismal anointing. (But that's not to say the person isn't fully baptized. He is.)

Light

A candle, lit from the Easter candle, signifies that Christ has enlightened the new Christian. In Jesus those who have been baptized are "the light of the world" (Mt 5:14; see Phil 2:15). We are called to share Christ's light with others.

The White Garment

The person being baptized dons a white garment to symbolize that she has "put on Christ" (Gal 3:27) and has risen with him.

At this point there's another difference between the sacrament's celebration in the East and in the West. In the West an adult receives confirmation and First Holy Communion, but an infant or young child doesn't. Instead, a child is brought to the altar for the praying of the Our Father. In the Eastern Churches, even the very young receive the Eucharist (in the form of wine, since a newborn can't swallow solid food) and are confirmed. (We'll talk more about that again in chapter three, on confirmation.)

The baptismal celebration concludes with a solemn blessing. At the baptisms of newborns there's a blessing of the mother.

The "ordinary ministers" of baptism are the bishop, priest,

and in the Latin Church, the deacon. But in case of necessity, anyone—even an unbaptized person—with the required intention can baptize by using the Trinitarian baptismal formula: "N., I baptize you in the name of the Father and of the Son and of the Holy Spirit. Amen."

What intention is required? The will to do what the Church does when it baptizes. The Church "finds the reason for this possibility in the universal saving will of God and the necessity of Baptism for salvation" (CCC 1256; see 1 Tm 2:4).

Can Non-Christians Enter Heaven?

"The necessity of Baptism for salvation" brings up an obvious question: Can only the baptized get to heaven? What about a devout Jew, Muslim, Hindu, Buddhist? What about a sincere and morally upright agnostic or atheist? (In the not-so-distant past, some even asked, "Can any non-Catholic enter heaven?")

In John 3:5 it's Jesus who says baptism is necessary for salvation. He's the one who commands his disciples to proclaim the gospel to all nations and baptize them (see Mt 28:19-20). So, the Church teaches, baptism is necessary for salvation for those to whom the gospel has been proclaimed and who have had the opportunity to ask for the sacrament (see Mk 16:16).

"The Church does not know of any means other than Baptism that assures entry into eternal beatitude [happiness]." However, "*God has bound salvation to the sacrament of Baptism, but he himself is not bound by his sacraments*" (CCC 1257).

Again, the development of doctrine can be seen here. There was a time when it was thought that unless a person was baptized, he or she could not enter heaven. This inspired great fear within families. Those who had been baptized believed that their unbaptized relatives would lose eternal happiness if they died without receiving the sacrament.

Missionaries charged with "saving souls" worked with great zeal to get as many people as possible baptized. Sad to say, in some instances politics and temporal powers were coupled with evangelization, and people were forced to submit to the ritual. Obviously, for any adult, baptism has to be a choice freely made. God invites but never forces.

At the same time, the Church has always said that those who are killed for the faith without being baptized are baptized by their death for and with Jesus. This is known as "baptism of blood." There is also "baptism of desire." For catechumens who die before receiving the sacrament, their explicit desire to receive it, together with repentance for their sins and charity, assures them the salvation they weren't able to receive through the sacrament.

Now the Church teaches that every person who is ignorant of the gospel and the Church but seeks the truth and does the will of God in accordance with his or her understanding of it can be saved. It may be supposed that the person would have desired baptism explicitly if he or she had known of its necessity.

What about children and infants who have died without being baptized? At one time the idea of "limbo" was commonly accepted. (The name came from the Latin *limbus,* meaning "hem" or "edge.") It could have been defined as "almost heaven." The Church never formally pronounced this idea as a dogma, an official teaching. Now it explicitly says that the Church can only entrust these souls to the mercy of God, as it does in their funeral rites. And it points out that the great mercy of God desires that all should be saved.

Furthermore, Jesus' tenderness toward children caused him to say, "Let the children come to me, do not hinder them" (Mk 10:14; see 1 Tm 2:4). That allows us "to hope that there is a way of salvation for children who have died without Baptism" (CCC 1261).

We leave it in God's hands. There's no better place it could be.

What *Really* Happens

We have presented the *how* and the *who* of baptism, but *what* is taking place? What's *really* happening?

Purification From Sins

All sins are forgiven, both original sin and personal sin, and all punishment for sin. Die immediately following baptism, and you're on the express to heaven. No stops along the way.

But baptism doesn't take away our free will. We still get to choose—and have to choose. In our sin-steeped world sin continues to hold its attraction. Even after we've been lifted to new life, we can choose the ways of death.

And most of us do. Time and time again. Catholics, you may have noticed, are not perfect. In the early Church this returning to sin was a particular concern. Should a baptized sinner be booted? Should a repentant baptized sinner be accepted back into the fold? Should that person be "rebaptized"? *Could* he or she be "rebaptized"?

We'll talk about the forgiveness of sins committed after baptism in chapter six, when we look at the sacrament of reconciliation. As for "rebaptizing," that can't happen. There is only *one* baptism, and a person can be baptized only *once.* Someone properly baptized in the Lutheran Church, or the Anglican Church—any Christian church—*is* baptized.

Because a person is "incorporated into Christ" by baptism, he or she is "configured" to Christ. This sacrament seals the Christian with the indelible mark—the "character"—of his or her belonging to Christ. There's no sin that can erase this mark, even if sin prevents baptism from "bearing the fruits of salvation." Given once for all, it can't be repeated.

"Baptism constitutes the foundation of communion among all Christians, including those who are not yet in full communion with the Catholic Church" (CCC 1271). Again, that's why at the Easter Vigil those candidates who were previously baptized—even baptized in another Christian denomination—make a profession of faith rather than receive the sacrament of baptism again.

We're Children of God

Baptism also makes the person "a new creation," an adopted child of God who has become a "partaker of the divine nature" (2 Cor 5:17; 2 Pt 1:4; see Gal 4:5-7), a member of Christ and coheir with him (see Rom 8:17), and a temple of the Holy Spirit (see 1 Cor 6:19).

The Holy Trinity gives the baptized sanctifying grace, the grace of "justification." That gift

- enables them to believe in God, to hope in him, and to love him through the theological virtues of faith, hope, and love

45

- gives them the power to live and act under the prompting of the Holy Spirit through the gifts of the Holy Spirit—traditionally, wisdom, understanding, knowledge, counsel, piety, fortitude, and fear of the Lord (We'll get back to them in the next chapter.)
- allows them to grow in goodness through the moral virtues

In this way and because of this, a Christian's supernatural life has its roots in baptism, and baptism makes him or her a member of the body of Christ. It incorporates a person into the Church. Being one of the people of God transcends all natural or human limits of nation, culture, race, or sex. "For by one Spirit we were all baptized into one body" (1 Cor 12:13).

Baptism makes us part of the community of saints—and of sinners. We join that pilgrim people sharing a communal lifestyle.

By baptism we also share in the priesthood of Christ and in his prophetic and royal mission. We no longer belong to ourselves but to him, and we're called to be of service to others and to obey and submit to the Church's leaders. With those responsibilities and duties come rights: to receive the sacraments, to be nourished by the Word of God, and to be sustained by the other spiritual helps of the Church.

We become another Christ. The name we bear—Christian—reminds us of our ministry to others. We don't live an individualistic lifestyle. We live for each other because we are sons and daughters of the same loving God.

Q & A: What's the Deal With Original Sin and With Godparents?

What was the "original sin"?
The first human beings chose their own will over God's will, and so they lost the grace of original holiness.

What do their actions have to do with me?
Humanity became subject to the law of death, and sin became universally present in the world. The term *original sin* also describes the fallen state of human nature, which affects every person born into this world.

Original sin isn't a physical ailment. It can be described as a state of chaos. Because of the act of Adam and Eve, we no longer knew who we were. We tried to be God. We tried to be Someone we were not. Baptism "orders" us again. It puts us back in order and lets a person know:

1. There is a God.
2. It's not you.

So if I'm baptized, that straightens everything out?
Yes and no. All sins are forgiven, but there are certain "temporal consequences" of sin. Those include suffering, illness, and even death itself. A list would also mention "human frailties" inherent in this world, such as weaknesses of character. Then, too, there's the inclination toward sin. Tradition calls this "concupiscence." It's

"'left for us to wrestle with ..., [but] it cannot harm those who do not consent but manfully resist it by the grace of Jesus Christ'" (CCC 1264; Council of Trent, 1546: DS 1515).

That's one reason each baptized person—infant, child, or adult—has a sponsor.

What's the difference between a sponsor and a godparent?
Same thing. Neither is meant to be simply an honorary role, although being asked to fulfill that role is a great honor. It's one that carries responsibilities.

At the baptism of an infant the godparent is questioned: "What do you ask of the Church?" The response is "Faith!" (A catechumen answers for himself or herself.) That faith must grow after receiving the sacrament. That's why each year at the Easter Vigil there's the renewal of baptismal promises for everyone.

For the graces of baptisms to unfold, a child needs a parent's help. A godfather and godmother, who must be firm believers, are also called upon to be able and ready to help the newly baptized on the road of Christian life. The sponsor's role is a specific ecclesial (Church) function. And the whole ecclesial community bears some responsibility for the development and safeguarding of the grace given at baptism.

More specifically, who can be a godparent?
A baptized, practicing Catholic sixteen years old or older who has received the sacraments of confirmation and Eucharist. Only one sponsor is required. Two, one of each sex, are permitted.

A non-Catholic Christian can't be a godparent for a Catholic child but may serve as a witness to the baptism. A Catholic can't be a godparent for a child baptized in a non-Catholic religion but may be a witness.

The role of godparents in the baptismal ceremonies is secondary to the role of the parents. The sponsors serve as representatives of the community of faith and, with the parents, request baptism for the child and perform other ritual functions. After baptism they serve as proxies for the parents if the parents should be unable to or fail to provide for the religious training of the child.

Does a Catholic have to take a saint's name at baptism?
While that's not mandatory, the Church recommends every child be given a name with Christian significance to symbolize newness of life in Christ.

THREE

Confirmation: Your Share in Pentecost

While every sacrament gives God's grace, confirmation is the one we most closely associate with the Holy Spirit. At confirmation "the Lord and Giver of Life" blows through our lives and brings his gifts in a unique way.

The Third Person of the Blessed Trinity can take a person to another level, as he offers the gifts Jesus had in full: wisdom, understanding, counsel, knowledge, piety, fortitude, and fear of the Lord. We get that list from Isaiah 11:1-3. *(Go to "A Fruit Basket From God," p. 62.)*

That's what the Spirit *offers*. That's what you can become more open to achieving. It's not that you suddenly have the ability to use those gifts to their full potential. You, too, play a role in developing that potential by recognizing what confirmation does and by using what it brings. It could be said confirmation gives spiritual "muscles" even as it further obligates the recipient to flex, build, and use those muscles.

This *Isn't* "Baptism II: The Sequel"

Confirmation is also a sacrament that's commonly misunderstood. Often it's seen as an opportunity for a child or teen to "confirm" his or her faith. ("OK, now that I'm older, I'll agree to the contract my parents signed in my name. Hand me a pen.") But its name refers to what the Church is doing as it confirms what took place at baptism. Although we are fully baptized, reception of the sacrament of confirmation is necessary for the completion of baptismal grace.

That's so because, to quote Vatican II's "Dogmatic Constitution on the Church," "incorporated in the Church through Baptism," Catholics "are more perfectly bound to the Church by the sacrament of Confirmation, and the Holy Spirit endows them with special strength so that they are more strictly obliged to spread and defend the faith, both by word and by deed, as true witnesses of Christ" (11).

Confirmation in Scripture

In the Old Testament the prophets foretold that the Spirit of the Lord would "rest on" the Messiah (see Is 11:2; 61:1). In the New Testament, at the beginning of his public ministry, Jesus announced, "Today this scripture has been fulfilled in your hearing " (Lk 4:21). In other words, "I am the one Isaiah was talking about."

Jesus' whole earthly life was intimately tied to the Spirit: from his conception, to his baptism by John, through his promise that, after his death, resurrection, and ascension, his heavenly Father would send the Spirit to the fledgling Church. It would be—it is—the same Father who had sent Jesus and given him the Spirit without measure—that is, completely (see Jn 3:34).

So this "fullness" of the Spirit was going to belong not only to Christ but to the whole messianic people—to all Christians. And it was that Spirit who blew through the upper room on Pentecost. Suddenly filled with his power, the till-then-timid apostles began to boldly proclaim "the mighty works of God," and Peter declared that this outpouring of the Spirit was a sign of the messianic age (Acts 2:11; see 2:17-18).

Those who heard Peter's preaching and were baptized received the gift of the Holy Spirit (see Acts 2:38), and then "the apostles, in fulfillment of Christ's will, imparted to the newly baptized by the laying on of hands, the gift of the Spirit that completes the grace of baptism" (Pope Paul VI, apostolic constitution titled "*Divinae consortium naturae*").

The Vatican II pontiff continued, "For this reason, in the Letters to the Hebrews the doctrine concerning Baptism and the laying on of hands is listed among the first elements of Christian instruction. The imposition of hands is rightly recognized by the Catholic tradition as the origin of the sacrament of Confirmation, which in a certain way perpetuates the grace of Pentecost in the Church."

It was also very early on that, to better signify the gift of the Spirit, an anointing with chrism (perfumed oil) was added. *(Go to "Q & A: What's Chrism, and Who's Myron?" p. 59.)* That has remained a part of the rite in both the East and the West, but even the names for the sacrament reflect a particular emphasis. In the East it's "chrismation," anointing with chrism. In the West "confirmation" is used to emphasize the fact that this sacrament confirms baptism and strengthens baptismal grace.

East Is East, and West Is West

As mentioned in the previous chapter, the East maintains that close tie among the three sacraments of initiation—baptism, confirmation, and Eucharist—by administering all of them at the same time, even in the case of infants and children. In the West the delay is seen as a way to underline the relationship between the one who is being baptized and the bishop, the successor of the apostles.

In the early centuries of the Church confirmation usually was part of a single celebration with baptism but not a single "sign." St. Cyprian (d. 258) referred to such an event as a "double sacrament." Why did the West develop two separate celebrations?

There were a number of reasons, including an increase in infant baptisms, more rural parishes, and the growth of dioceses. The result was that, more and more frequently, a bishop wasn't able to be present at all baptisms.

There were two solutions. In the East the priest conferred confirmation at baptism. In the West the desire to reserve the completion of baptism to the bishop meant a separation of the two sacraments. But even in the East the priest can confirm only with oil consecrated by a bishop.

Signs and Forms

When baptism and confirmation are celebrated separately, the liturgy of confirmation begins with the renewal of baptismal promises and the profession of faith by the "confirmands" (or to use the old Latin term, *"confirmandi"*).

The bishop—or a "vicar," a priest the bishop designates to act in his place—extends his hands over those to be confirmed. Since apostolic times this has been a gesture that signifies the gift of the Spirit. The sacrament is conferred through the anointing of chrism on the forehead, which is done by the laying on of the hands and through the words "Be sealed with the gift of the Holy Spirit."

In the Eastern Churches of the Byzantine rite, after a prayer of epiclesis—that calling down of the Holy Spirit—it isn't just the head that is anointed but the forehead, eyes, nose, ears, lips, chest, back, hands, and feet. With each anointing the celebrant says, "The seal of the gift of the Holy Spirit."

In the West, the rite of confirmation concludes with the sign of peace, to show the relationship with the bishop and with all the community. Older Catholics may remember that at one time the rite included the bishop's giving each confirmand a slight tap on the cheek. Its symbolism got muddied over the years. Originally more of a fatherly caress—a sign of peace—it came to be seen as a reminder that "now you gotta grow up and be tough." The tap on the cheek is no longer part of the liturgy.

The custom of choosing a "confirmation name" has come to symbolize the "new" person. A Church council in the sixteenth century advised that someone whose name was "vile, ridiculous, or quite unbecoming for a Christian" should take another one. While a person is still free to do that, the thinking now is that sticking with the baptismal name better expresses the relationship between the two sacraments.

Who Should Be Confirmed?

Every baptized person in good standing with the Church who hasn't been confirmed can be and should be. Canon Law points out that since the three sacraments of initiation form a unity, "the faithful are obliged to received this sacrament at the appropriate time" (Canon 890). Again, without confirmation and Eucharist, baptism is valid and efficacious (there's that word again; it means it always brings the result it says it will), but a Christian's "initiation" remains incomplete.

While the East continues to confirm infants, what's the "right age" in the West? In recent times it has slid between about eight and eighteen. The benchmark remains "the age of discretion"—the age at which a person can tell right from wrong—but the question is, How soon after that?

The bishops of the United States have yet to establish a national uniform policy. Some places have begun to have confirmation even before First Communion. Many continue to make it a milestone for eighth-graders, while others see it almost as a rite of passage for high school students.

At any age—for a child, teen, or adult—preparation for the sacrament aims at leading the person toward a more intimate union with Christ and an increased familiarity with the Holy Spirit, his actions and gifts—and his promptings, his "biddings."

Coming to better know and love Jesus and the Spirit is important, part of the foundation of the apostolic responsibilities of Christian life. All God's people are called to be "messengers" (apostles!) of the Good News by their words and their actions. That's also why the confirmand's preparation involves better understanding the fact that he or she belongs not just to a parish or local faith community but to a universal Church, to the Church of Jesus Christ.

The Sponsor's Role

Helping the confirmand prepare not just for reception of the sacrament but for "living" it afterward is part of the job description for the sponsor. That's why, to again quote the Code of Canon Law, "as far as possible a sponsor for the one to be confirmed should be present; it is for the sponsor to see that the confirmed person acts as a true witness to Christ and faithfully fulfills the obligations connected with the sacrament" (Canon 892).

The requirements for a confirmation sponsor are the same as those for a sponsor at baptism. It's "desirable," the Code points out, that the baptismal sponsor also be the sponsor at confirmation. Again, being a sponsor isn't an honorary role or title, although it is an honor to have someone choose you for a sponsor. It brings with it obligations because the sacrament itself does the same.

"Special Effects" From Here to Eternity

As the Catechism explains, confirmation has a number of effects:

• It roots a person more deeply in the parent-child relationship with God (as we pray, "Abba! Daddy!").

- It unites the person more firmly to Christ.
- It increases the gifts of the Holy Spirit within the person.
- It renders the person's bond to the Church more perfect.
- It gives the person a special strength of the Holy Spirit to spread and defend the faith by word and action as a true witness of Christ, to confess the name of Christ boldly, and to never be ashamed of the cross. (Again, this was why, in recent times past, the bishop's slap was interpreted by many as "Get tough, here's what's headed your way.")

As with baptism and holy orders (which we'll look at in chapter eight), the sacrament of confirmation imprints an indelible spiritual mark on the soul. That "character" is the sign that Jesus has marked this person with the seal of the Spirit, by "clothing him with power from on high so that he may be his witness" (CCC 1304).

Confirmation also perfects the "common priesthood" of the faithful, which was received in baptism. Now the person is given the power to profess Christ publicly and "officially." The Latin term for this is *quasi ex officio.* It entails being involved in ministry, letting the gifts and fruits of the Spirit show in oneself, and taking leadership in the Church community.

Just as baptism is our rising from the dead with Christ, confirmation puts us in the upper room on that first Pentecost. The same Spirit leads us out into the world and hands us the gifts—the tools—we need to boldly proclaim the Good News.

Q & A: What's Chrism, and Who's Myron?

Why does the Church use oil?
In the Old Testament, kings, priests, and once in awhile, prophets were anointed. In ancient times oil was a sign of abundance and joy. It was used for cleaning (both before and after a bath) and for limbering up (athletes slathered it on). It was a symbol of healing because it was used to soothe bruises and wounds. And then as now, it was thought of as a cosmetic, adding beauty as well as health and strength.

What does that have to do with confirmation?
Anointing has to do with all those meanings when it's used in a sacrament. There's the pre-baptismal anointing with the "oil of catechumens," which signifies cleansing and strengthening; the anointing of the sick with the "oil of the sick" to show healing and comfort; and the use of sacred chrism for the post-baptismal anointing and at confirmation and ordination as a sign of consecration.

What's the difference between the "oil of catechumens," "oil of the sick," and "sacred chrism"?
Each can be olive or vegetable oil and is blessed by the bishop, normally during Holy Week. Also, each of these three sacramentals is used in a particular way.

"Chrism" has balm mixed with it. Also called "balsam," balm is a thick, aromatic tree resin that was once prized for both its pleasant smell and its assumed medicinal properties. In Old Testament times, anointing a king or priest with it symbolized his goodness and healing presence in the community.

The oil of catechumens is used for infants within the baptismal rite and for children and adults in the catechumen process.

The oil of the sick is used for the sacrament of the sick. (This isn't the non-sacramental oil sometimes used at prayer meetings for healing.) Through this anointing the Church commends those who are ill to Christ and asks for physical and spiritual healing. The sacrament must be performed by a priest.

Oil is also used for certain blessings, such as the dedications of churches and altars.

In some Eastern Churches only the patriarch consecrates the holy oil. (The pope is the "patriarch" of the Roman Church.) The prayer of consecration in the liturgy of Antioch—the "epiclesis"—recaps and reminds the congregation about oil's symbolism:

[Father, ... send your Holy Spirit] on us and on this oil which is before us and consecrate it, so that it may be for all who are anointed and marked with it, holy myron, priestly myron, royal myron, anointing with gladness, clothing with light, a cloak of salvation, a spiritual gift, the sanctification of souls and bodies, imperishable happiness, the indelible seal, a buckler of faith, and a fearsome helmet against all the works of the adversary.

Who's "the adversary"?
Satan.

Who's "Myron"?
"Myron" is a "what," not a "who." It's the Eastern name for chrism.

Is all this ancient history?
Yes, but it's not limited to the past. The basic word used to describe our religion refers to our being anointed.

How's that?
That's what *Christian* means. It obviously comes from *Christ,* whom God "anointed with the Holy Spirit" (Acts 10:38). *Christ* isn't Jesus' last name. It is a title and a description. He was (and is) "the Christ," *the* Anointed One.

We get *Christ* from the Greek translation of the Hebrew *Messiah.* They mean the same. *Christ* became his "name" because he perfectly accomplished his divine mission as priest, prophet, and king.

Where is this Church oil kept?
You've probably seen it but may not have known what it was. Or you may have noticed where it was reserved in the past.

After Holy Thursday's "Chrism Mass" all three kinds of oils are distributed to parishes. Typically they're stored in three nice bottles up by the altar or near the baptismal font. A small amount can be transferred to a receptacle for use during the celebration of a sacrament.

There was a time when the three oils were kept in an "ambry," a locked wall cupboard. Some older church buildings still have a little door in the sanctuary wall that's marked "*Olea Sancta,*" the Latin for "holy oils."

A Fruit Basket From God

The Holy Spirit doesn't put a bow on his gifts, but he does always personalize them. What are these gifts?

In the fifth century Pope St. Gregory summed them up this way: "The Holy Spirit gives wisdom against folly, understanding against dullness, counsel against rashness, fortitude against fears, knowledge against ignorance, piety against hardness of our heart, and fear against pride."

At the beginning of the twentieth century "The Catholic Encyclopedia" offered this explanation of each:

The gift of wisdom, by detaching us from the world, makes us relish and love only the things of heaven.

The gift of understanding helps us to grasp the truths of religion as far as is necessary.

The gift of counsel springs from supernatural prudence and enables us to see and choose correctly what will help most to the glory of God and our own salvation.

By the gift of fortitude we receive courage to overcome the obstacles and difficulties that arise in the practice of our religious duties.

The gift of knowledge points out to us the path to follow and the dangers to avoid in order to reach heaven.

The gift of piety, by inspiring us with a tender and filial confidence in God, makes us joyfully embrace all that pertains to his service.

Lastly, the gift of fear fills us with a sovereign respect for God and makes us dread, above all things, to offend him.

What about the "fruits of the Holy Spirit"? The Church says they're the "perfections" the Holy Spirit forms in us as the "first fruits" of eternal glory. We get the list from Galatians 5:22-23, and it includes love, joy, peace, patience, kindness, goodness, faithfulness, gentleness, and self-control.

FOUR

Eucharist: Your Best Meal Ever

Baptism and confirmation aren't just once-in-a-lifetime events but once-in-eternity celebrations. Eucharist is the ongoing sacrament of initiation. It's the one that we can receive over and over again, as it calls us to go more deeply into the mystery of God's love and the mystery of God's presence.

"Holy Communion" deepens our relationship with Christ, and it connects us to both the community here on earth and the saints in heaven. It prefigures the "heavenly banquet"; it is, as the early Church put it, "the bread of the eighth day" because with this sacrament, we step out of natural time and into eternal time.

The Eucharist "is the source and summit of the Christian life," the bishops wrote in their Vatican II document "Dogmatic Constitution on the Church" (11). In their "Decree on the Ministry and Life of Priests" they explained that "the other sacraments, and indeed all ecclesiastical ministries and works of the apostolate, are bound up in the Eucharist and are oriented toward it. For in the blessed Eucharist is contained the whole spiritual good of the Church, namely Christ himself, our Pasch" (5).

Pasch means "Paschal lamb." The One who gave his life on Calvary is the same One who is present—body and soul, humanity and divinity—in the Blessed Sacrament. Jesus is in the Eucharist, always, for you.

What's in a Name?

Eucharist. Holy Communion. Blessed Sacrament. It's not surprising this sacrament has a lot of names; there's a lot to it, and a single word or phrase is too limiting. Examining some of the names for it, which are really descriptions of it, can help us better understand what it is we hold in the palm of our hand at Mass—actually, *whom* we hold.

We hold God.

Obviously, we can't completely understand this. But we are able to lessen our misunderstanding and, in doing so, better appreciate this sacrament. The more we learn about it, through God's grace at work in our efforts, the more it can amaze us. It can fill our minds, our hearts, and our souls.

Eucharist

As with so many of our "Church words," *Eucharist* comes from Greek. At its roots it means "thanksgiving." In this sacrament, through this sacrament, by this sacrament, we thank God. For what? Creation (he made everything, including us); redemption (he sent his Son to save us from our sins); and sanctification (he brings us to our heavenly home).

The Lord's Supper

Christ instituted this sacrament at the Last Supper, the final meal he shared with his apostles before his passion, death, and resurrection. The first "Mass" was on that Holy Thursday evening, and it's in the Mass that bread and wine become Christ's body. This name also refers to the Eucharist's "anticipating" the heavenly banquet, "the marriage supper of the Lamb" in the heavenly Jerusalem (see Rv 19:9).

The Breaking of Bread

The first Mass was part of a Jewish meal, and Jesus, as the head person at that table, blessed, broke, and distributed bread. After the Resurrection his followers recognized the risen Lord in "the breaking of the bread" (see Lk 24:13-35). This is the phrase the early Church used to refer to eucharistic assemblies (the first-century equivalent of our Sunday Masses). It's the term used in the Acts of the Apostles (2:42, 46; 20:7, 11).

What does this term signify? According to St. Paul, those who eat this broken bread enter into communion with Christ and form one body in him: "The bread which we break, is it not a participation in the body of Christ? Because there is one bread, we who are many are one body, for we all partake of the one bread" (1 Cor 10:17).

Eucharistic Assembly (or Synax)

This name isn't as common among folks in the pew in our own time. It refers to the fact that the sacrament is celebrated among the assembly of the faithful and is the visible expression of the Church.

The Holy and Divine Liturgy

It's in the celebration of the Eucharist that the Church's whole liturgy finds its center and most intense expression.

Sacred Mysteries

It has been called this for the same reason.

Most Blessed Sacrament

This is "the sacrament of sacraments," so the Eucharist reserved in the tabernacle is called this.

Holy Communion

By this sacrament we unite ourselves to Christ, who makes us sharers in his Body and Blood to form one body. Remember St. Paul's words to the Corinthians: "The cup of blessing which we bless, is it not a participation in the blood of Christ?" (10:16).

Holy Mass

The liturgy in which the bread and wine become the Body and Blood of Christ concludes with a sending out of the faithful to fulfill God's will in their daily lives. In Latin this is *missio*. *Mass* and *missionary* have the same root.

Other Names

The holy things, the communion of saints (a phrase that has another meaning, too: the faithful on earth, in heaven, and in purgatory), *the bread of angels, bread from heaven, medicine of immortality* (that one's not used much these days), and *viaticum*. That last one is the final reception of the Eucharist before death. We'll talk about that a little later.

Why Have Mass?

What really happens at Mass? What really happens to those wafers of bread that don't look or taste like our everyday bread? What really happens to that wine?

Maybe before we ask those questions, we should consider some that are even more basic: Why do we have the Mass? Why do we use bread and wine? Why do we do what we do, and why did Jesus do what he did? Not just giving us himself in this way (although that's not really "just," is it?) but giving us himself in this way by this method.

In a single sentence: At the heart of the Mass are the bread and wine that, by the words of Christ and the invocation of the Holy Spirit, become Christ's Body and Blood. This is something we're supposed to do. It isn't something that we simply might want to try or something that's even highly recommended. Jesus said to do it, to do this in his memory until he comes back at the end of time.

How and when he gave us this command, this incredible gift, underscore both the command and the gift. It was at the last meal he ate before he was arrested, beaten, and executed. He knew what was coming. He knew it was one of his own, one of his handpicked "messengers," who would tell the authorities where and when they could find him—the place and the time to grab him with only a few others nearby.

So much happened from Thursday evening until Sunday dawn that we, the Church, are still examining it. There is layer upon layer upon layer. Again, because of the development of doctrine, we in our time have the advantage of almost two thousand years of the Holy Spirit's helping the holiest and the brightest among us reflect on those sixty or so hours.

That same Spirit helps each of us look at those layers. We have opportunities through both prayer and study to delve deeper into the reality of the Mass, of the Eucharist—to explore and consider and meditate on Christ's passion, death, and resurrection.

At their very core, all those events are bound together. All are our salvation. Even as we learn more and better appreciate what happened and what continues to happen—what, incredibly, is available to each of us—we come to the greater realization that we're never going to completely "get it." That's so because at the very core of all these events is an infinite God.

He's our infinite God—"ours" not because we chose him but because he chose us. And that choosing began long before Christ's birth. God spent centuries preparing humanity for the arrival of the Second Person of the Blessed Trinity, because humanity needed a lot of preparing. We had shown incredible creativity in messing up creation. We still do.

Our Jewish Roots

At Sunday Mass, at every Mass, the priest says, "He took bread," and, "He took the cup filled with wine." The celebrant describes what Jesus did at the Last Supper. We get those accounts from the "synoptic Gospels" (Matthew, Mark, and Luke, so called because of their similarity), while John gives us other insights into that special meal. Another primary source is Paul's First Letter to the Corinthians. *(Go to "Q & A: Was There a Collection at the First Mass?" p. 75.)*

What we may not realize, what we can easily forget, is that the priest's words are describing a first-century Jewish celebration. According to the synoptics, it was a Passover meal. This type of celebration was taking place in homes throughout Palestine on that night, just as in our own time Jews annually celebrate Passover dinner—the "seder"—with friends and family.

Here's a comparison. Someone begins a new and wonderful tradition at a Thanksgiving dinner. This new event gains popularity, and over time, its connection to the November holiday fades. At the new celebration—by now, no longer considered "new"—there's turkey and cranberry sauce. Those are used because, well, those are used. Most celebrants don't think about why those items are on the menu, but interestingly enough, other folks who don't celebrate this new event but have kept having Thanksgiving use the same two foods at their celebration. Huh. Quite a coincidence.

But it isn't a coincidence. And it isn't a coincidence that the Mass and the Passover meal are similar. The Passover celebrated the old covenant (agreement) between God and his chosen people. It reminded them of who they were, where they were, and what Yahweh did to get them back to where they not only wanted to be but truly belonged.

Even as it is celebrated today, the Passover meal—the seder—is about being led from slavery in Egypt to freedom in Israel. The prayers, the actions, the items on the menu in the first century and the twenty-first, focus on the Exodus.

The Mass celebrates the new covenant between God and his Church. But more than simply reminding us of who we are, where we are, and what the Father, Son, and Spirit have done to get us back to where we truly want to be and truly belong, it makes present in a particular and tangible way the very One who instituted the sacrament: the One who dined with his apostles on that Thursday night; the One who was ratted out, grabbed up, mocked, tortured, and slowly and painfully executed; the One who really died and really came back to life; the One who ascended to his heavenly Father; the One who told his still-baffled followers that the Father would send the Spirit of love, who has always existed between the two of them.

It's that resurrected Christ who is present in the Eucharist under the appearances of bread and wine—at every Mass, every time. *(Go to "Bleeding Hosts and Hocus-Pocus," p. 77.)*

The Chosen Menu

In the old covenant, bread and wine were offered in sacrifice along with "first fruits" of the earth to thank the Creator. In Genesis 14:18 the king-priest Melchizedek "brought out bread and wine," and that, the Church says, "prefigured" what happens at the Mass. Even the descriptions used now— "work of human hands," "fruit of the earth" and "of the vine" in the Offertory of the Mass—echo Psalm 104:13-15: "The earth is satisfied with the fruit of thy work. Thou dost ... bring forth food from the earth, and wine to gladden the heart of man."

After the chosen people returned to the Promised Land, there was new symbolism. The unleavened (without yeast) bread of the Passover commemorated the haste with which the Israelites had had to leave Egypt. It also became a reminder of the manna the Lord had provided in the desert.

"He humbled you and let you hunger and fed you with manna, which you did not know, nor did your fathers know; that he might make you know that man does not live by bread alone, but that man lives by everything that proceeds out of the mouth of the Lord" (Dt 8:3).

Once they had returned to Israel, their daily bread was the "fruit" of the Promised Land. It was a pledge of God's faithfulness to his promises.

The wine, too, was (and is) an integral part of the Passover meal. The "cup of blessing" (1 Cor 10:16), offered at the end of the seder, was supposed to gladden the human heart as it gave an "eschatological" dimension to the celebration. ("Eschatological" means having to do with the end of time.) At the conclusion of the Passover meal, thoughts turned to anticipation of the Messiah, coming to rebuild Jerusalem. At the Last Supper, in the Eucharist, Jesus put yet another "twist" on this. The Messiah had come. He instituted this sacrament, and he said, "Keep doing this until I come again."

So we keep doing it until the Messiah comes a final time.

Some Hints From Jesus

Just as bread blessed, broken, and given, wine offered and shared, didn't come out of the blue at the Last Supper, Jesus tipped his hand during his public ministry. Looking back after Pentecost, the apostles and others came to realize that the Son of God was doing more than feeding the multitudes with a few loaves of bread and a couple of fish (see Mt 14:13-21; 15:32-39).

Those were unforgettable events, without a doubt, but—as is so often the case with what Jesus said and did—they were more than that. Feeding thousands from a bit of bread and a couple of fish prefigured the superabundance of that one-of-a-kind bread we call the Eucharist. That bread has fed millions and will continue to feed millions. That bread has been blessed, broken, and distributed for almost two thousand years.

Wine, too, played a role in Jesus' public ministry. At the wedding feast at Cana, in his first miracle, ordinary water in ordinary water jugs became the finest vintage (see Jn 2:1-11). This is where and when and how the Anointed One's public ministry began. For centuries the Jews had been raising a cup and dreaming of the day the Messiah would appear. When he made his presence known publicly, he supplied the wine. This round was on him.

At the great wedding feast that never ends—in heaven—the faithful will drink the new wine that has become the very Blood of Christ.

Jesus told the people they would eat his body and drink his blood, and the people, being sensible and intelligent, said, "Eat his *what* and drink his *what!*" It was terrific to see him comfort, feed, and cure folks. Who wouldn't want to at least go see him when he was in the area, if not actually go on the road with him? Who wouldn't—if a son or daughter was sick, if a spouse was hurting, if a parent was near death—ask for help, with an understandable combination of desperation and faith? Who wouldn't be astounded by reports that he had actually brought the dead back to life?

But "Eat my body"? "Drink my blood"?

Not a few people concluded he had, well, gone over the

top. He had lost it. He was severely deluded if not downright insane. Who, other than a madman, would talk of such cannibalism?

The sixth chapter of John's Gospel begins with the feeding of the multitude and ends with Jesus' "difficult" teaching. Because of that teaching, "many of his disciples drew back and no longer went about with him" (v. 66). He asked the twelve, "What about you?" And Peter answered, "Lord, to whom can we go? You have the words of eternal life. We have come to believe and know you are the Holy One of God."

The apostles didn't understand what Jesus was talking about. They certainly couldn't explain it to others. But they believed. The same is true today for all Catholics. We don't understand it. We certainly can't explain it to others. But we believe.

In the next chapter we'll take a closer look at the Mass and "transubstantiation."

Q & A: Was There a Collection at the First Mass?

Was there a collection at the first Mass? (Just kidding.)
The evangelists and St. Paul don't mention one. (No kidding.)

On the other hand, the generosity of the people was a central element of that group that gathered for the breaking of the bread.

Do those five writers—Matthew, Mark, Luke, John, and Paul—say the same thing about the first Mass?

Yes and no. They present the same incredible truth, but how they do that varies. The synoptics (Mt 26:17-29; Mk 14:12-25; Lk 22:7-20) include the first Eucharist at the Last Supper. Paul's report of that event is similar (1 Cor 11:23-25).

It's John who has a different presentation, as he often does. In his Gospel Jesus had already called himself the Bread of Life in the synagogue in Capernaum (in chapter six). At John's Last Supper scene, Jesus—the ultimate servant—washed the feet of the apostles as a sign of his love (Jn 13:1-17, 34-35.) Even in our own time, when the Church celebrates the liturgy on the evening of Holy Thursday, there is the washing of feet. The main celebrant—whether he is a priest, bishop, cardinal, or pope—does this.

Where was Capernaum?

In the north. In modern language, it was the sticks. Jesus—born in Bethlehem, which is less than ten miles from Jerusalem—was brought up in Nazareth, another northern town. It, too, was considered the sticks. Jesus was a small-town boy who went to the Big City.

Why don't all those New Testament accounts agree?

Each writer, inspired by the Holy Spirit, had a particular style and was emphasizing particular points to particular audiences. That's true for all the authors of Scripture (see CCC 106-7).

Anything else?
One more point. The Last Supper was also where Jesus instituted the priesthood. We look at holy orders in chapter eight.

Bleeding Hosts and Hocus-Pocus

It might be tempting to think we use the word "host" for the Communion wafer because "Jesus is our host, and we are his guests," but we get the word from the Latin *hostia,* meaning "victim."

Jesus was, and is, the victim on the cross and at the "unbloody sacrifice of the Mass." The Mass isn't a reenactment of Calvary but a re-presentation: It makes that event present again. The sacrifice of Christ and the sacrifice of the Eucharist are one single sacrifice.

As Church historians (and magicians) are fond of pointing out, in the Middle Ages the words of consecration in Latin, *hoc est enim corpus meum* ("For this is my body"), were mocked by some as "hocus-pocus." Folks caught the priest's "hoc est" and added the "pocus." That flat bread becomes God? What a hoot!

At a time when alchemists were diligently trying to turn lead into gold—which, if it worked, would be a real money-maker—it wasn't too difficult to ridicule the idea of unleavened bread becoming the true Body of Christ.

Needless to say, through the centuries, relatively sincere experiments were done on the consecrated host by some skeptics. And poignant acts of desecration were committed by those who violently opposed the Church.

Then, too, pious legends arose of bleeding hosts and pulsing hosts and hosts that took on human form in all sorts of what we today would consider bizarre if not downright gory ways. The Church doesn't say a Catholic must believe those stories, no matter how commonly accepted they were then— or are now among some devout people. That's so even in the truly miraculous instances.

What the Church does say and teach is that, to repeat a very important point, the forms of bread and wine do not change, but both are altered in substance. Both undergo transubstantiation. We'll talk about that next.

FIVE

Eucharist, Continued:
Your Presence Is Requested

It bears repeating that a miracle is at the heart of the Mass. Just as way back when Jesus' words about eating his flesh and drinking his blood had some people shaking their heads and walking away, what the Church teaches about that wafer of bread and chalice of wine troubles folks today.

It just doesn't seem—it just can't be—right. The claim is just too much. Then and now, what happens seems incredible. The old spiritual says, "He's got the whole world in his hands." And you have him in yours.

Looks Can Be Deceiving

In the early Church there wasn't even a word for what happens. It was only with the development of the doctrine on the Eucharist that the term *transubstantiation* began being used. It means that through the consecration of the bread and wine there's a change of the entire substance of the bread into the Body of Christ and the entire substance of the wine into the Blood of Christ.

That happens even though the appearance or "species" of bread and wine remain. They feel, look, taste, and smell the same. Someone who is allergic to wheat will have an allergic reaction to the consecrated host. Someone who drinks consecrated wine will have the same blood-alcohol reading as if he drank that amount of unconsecrated wine.

Making this even more confusing, we continue to use the words "bread" and "wine" after both have been consecrated. But, the Church says, they really aren't those anymore. In this Blessed Sacrament, as the Council of Trent (1545–63) put it: "The body and blood, together with the soul and divinity, of Our Lord Jesus Christ and, therefore, the whole Christ is truly, really, and substantially contained" (DS 1651).

Referring to this as the "Real Presence" doesn't mean other types of presences are not real. It means Jesus' presence in the fullest sense. It is a "substantial" (one of substance) presence by which Jesus, the true God and a human being, makes himself wholly and entirely present.

From the Scientific Perspective

While the Catholic Church, East and West, uses countless symbols and has since its earliest years, the Blessed Sacrament isn't one of them. In the Eucharist, God is not a symbol for God. God is God.

In our own time, a growing number of Catholics are unfamiliar with the concept of the Real Presence and the doctrine of transubstantiation. The bishops have voiced concern that the idea of "symbol only" is being accepted because of both a lack of fundamental religious education and a surrender to personal preference. Then, too, there remains the "If I can't understand it, I'm not going to believe it" mentality.

That latter approach often asks for cold, hard facts that are provable by science. "If you cannot prove to me that ..., then I do not believe that ..." But while we live on earth, God's presence—in the Eucharist, in our souls, in our lives, in his kingdom that's already among us—can't be proven in that way.

That doesn't mean science and religion are supposed to be at odds. Both, at their best, focus on the truth. Science searches for the truth in the physical. Religion says that what science discovers offers further proof of an infinite, all-powerful, truly marvelous, and awe-inspiring God who created the physical.

Accepting the faith and living the faith requires faith. And faith, the Church teaches, is also a gift from God. It's one that we're called on to nurture through prayer and study.

Then, too, it's important to keep in mind that the gift requires a healthy skepticism as well as a holy humility. We're obligated to ask our questions if we have them and search for answers, even as we recognize that at some point in our search we're going to have to admit that God—and what he does and how he does it—is beyond our feeble little minds.

Again, that describes the Eucharist. We come to that point at every Mass, from the loftiest Easter celebration in St. Peter's Basilica in Rome to a weekday service at a mission parish in the most remote corner of the world. Jesus becomes present. The bread and wine become Jesus.

And that's true no matter what we think of the particular Mass we attend. The liturgy is designed to enhance what is taking place, but whether we find a particular Mass "good" or "bad," whether it appeals to us or not, whether its music, vestments, preaching, and all the rest would be considered world-class or bare-bones, the Eucharist "works."

The Roles of the Priest and the People

It's God who changes the wafer and wine into Christ. And he does that in a particular way with particular ministers because, well, that's how he set it up.

Again, the Church didn't "invent" any of the sacraments. They were handed to us within a framework. For the Eucharist, it was the Last Supper. That wasn't just the "first Mass"; it was also the institution of the ministers who would preside over the Mass: priests.

We'll talk more about the sacrament of holy orders in chapter eight, but we need to take a glance at the ordained ministry now because it's central and vital to the Eucharist. They literally go hand in hand. It's within the priest's hands that the host and wine become Christ. It's from the priest's hands, or the hands of his designated Eucharistic minister, that Christ is placed in our hands.

In the fourth century St. John Chrysostom wrote: "It is not man that causes the things offered to become the Body and Blood of Christ, but he who was crucified for us, Christ himself. The priest, in the role of Christ, pronounces these words, but their power and grace are God's. This is my body, he says. This word transforms the things offered."

Again, as with all the sacraments, the Eucharist doesn't somehow depend on the priest's being a terrific and holy person. He well may be. But because the sacrament is efficacious and because in his ordained role he acts *in persona Christi*—in the person of Christ—that isn't a prerequisite as he presides at the celebration.

None of this means that members of the congregation are

supposed to just "sit on their hands." The community of baptized people at the celebration, "by regeneration and the anointing of the Holy Spirit, are consecrated to be a spiritual house and a holy priesthood, that through all the works of Christian men they may offer spiritual sacrifices" ("Dogmatic Constitution on the Church," 10; see 1 Pt 2:4-5). All the baptized share that "common priesthood" in the sole priest, Christ. That's why the Mass is not a spectator event, even though sometimes how a particular liturgy is celebrated is spectacular.

As the Vatican II bishops wrote in the "Constitution on the Sacred Liturgy": "Mother Church earnestly desires that all the faithful should be led to that full, conscious, and active participation in liturgical celebrations which is demanded by the very nature of the liturgy, and to which the Christian people, 'a chosen race, a royal priesthood, a holy nation, a redeemed people' (1 Pt 2:9, 4-5), have a right and obligation by reason of their baptism" ("Constitution on the Sacred Liturgy," 14).

But "all the members do not have the same function" (Rom 12:4). Particular ones are called by God—in and through the Church—to a special service. They're chosen and consecrated by the sacrament of holy orders, by which the Spirit enables them to act *in persona Christi*.

Then and Now

The *Catechism* explains that since it's in the Eucharist that the sacrament of the Church is made visible, it's in the bishop's presiding at it that his ministry is most evident, as well as, in communion with him, the ministry of priests and deacons.

We are, and always have been, an "apostolic Church." (In the Nicene Creed, said at Sunday Mass, we pronounce our belief in the four "marks"—characteristics—of the Church: one, holy, Catholic, and apostolic.) The bishops are the successors of the apostles, part of an unbroken lineage that goes back to the Last Supper.

There are other particular ministries for the non-ordained. Those functions are determined by the bishop, in line with liturgical traditions and pastoral needs, and would include Eucharistic ministers, altar servers, readers, commentators, and choir members. Each serves "a genuine liturgical function" ("Constitution on the Sacred Liturgy," 29).

While some of those functions would seem foreign to first-century Christians, the "breaking of the bread" then and now follows the same outline. Of course, at the heart of it—at the heart of the Church—are the forms and signs of this sacrament: the consecration of the bread and wine.

In the middle of the second century St. Justin wrote a description of the Eucharistic celebration that, by and large, could be Sunday Mass at any parish in the twenty-first century. It concludes with members of the congregation being given Communion to take to "those who are absent."

Even in the time of the apostles, the Mass (and this was long before it was called the Mass) wasn't just that central point for the community of believers. It wasn't just the pinnacle of the community's week. It was a starting point, a jumping-off point.

Go!

They devoted themselves to the apostles' teaching and fellowship, to the breaking of bread and the prayers.... And all who believed were together and had all things in common; and they sold their possessions and goods and distributed them to all, as any had need. And day by day, attending the temple together and breaking bread in their homes, they partook of food with glad and generous hearts, praising God and having favor with all the people. And the Lord added to their number day by day those who were being saved.

ACTS 2:42, 44-47

The early Christians didn't forget Jesus' washing the apostles' feet. The "Eucharistic lifestyle" means being called to a life of service, then and now. In our own time we sometimes use "social justice" to describe one facet of that lifestyle. While a few of us are called to a solitary vocation—in a hermitage or cloister—the Eucharist says, "Go out into the marketplace." Sharing the Good News means bringing Christ to others as well as bringing them to Christ. One way we do that is through service. (And of course, by serving them we are serving Jesus; see Matthew 25:31-46.)

Then, too, those called to that hermitage or cloister serve others—including us!—through their prayers on our behalf.

The point is that there has never been a separation of prayer and action in the Church. The "Eucharistic lifestyle" has always had both—and demands both—because, again, that's how Jesus set it up. *He* washed those dirty feet. *He* blessed that bread and wine. *He* told us to do what he had done.

Your Table Is Ready

In a sense, what Jesus did was offer us a seat at three tables: our home, our parish, and our eternal reward, heaven.

There can be a eucharistic nature in our home as we gather at the dining table. At meals there can be that sense of love and thanksgiving, along with service. (Whose night to do the dishes?) As we say a simple grace, we are that "two or three gathered in Jesus' name," and he is in our midst (Mt 18:20).

Just as we may seldom think of our dining room table as an altar, we may too infrequently remember that the altar in our parish church is a dining room table. The first Mass was at a supper in a house. The very early Church had no church buildings. There were "domestic churches": homes at which the Eucharist was celebrated. (*Go to "Keep Holy the Lord's Day,"* p. 91.)

And it may be even more rare that we think about the eternal banquet. In our oh-so-limited speculation on what heaven is really like, we seldom consider this image of the banquet, which Jesus used and which is prominent in Scripture. It will be the feast that never ends, with people whom we love and who love us, great food and drink.

Because Jesus has redeemed us—has saved us from our own stupid, selfish actions—we can have a seat at that table. Because Jesus gave himself to us in a particular way in the Eucharist, we can catch a glimpse of what that spectacular dinner party will be like. What's on the menu here is the main dish there: Jesus, the Bread of Life.

We're called to eat at all three tables. We can accept or ignore those invitations. We can answer or toss that divine R.S.V.P. Church law requires us to receive Holy Communion at least once a year during the Easter season—from Easter Sunday to Pentecost. This "Easter Duty" is a reminder from the Church to take advantage of God's gift in the Eucharist.

One way we can choose to respond is through our full and active participation in the liturgy. We can choose to not just "go to Mass" but to really "be at Mass."

Christ has promised he will be present there, and he always is. Even as we sit in a pew, stand, and kneel, we determine how "present" we are.

Q & A: Why Can't Protestants Receive Holy Communion?

Why can't Protestants receive Holy Communion?
The Eucharist is an area in which there are clear differences among Christian traditions, but it can be confusing because Protestants and Catholics use a lot of the same terminology. Catholicism says the bread and wine become Jesus. Some Protestants believe this also, but many Protestant churches teach that both remain symbols only. Even those who do believe in the Real Presence are not invited to receive Communion in the Catholic Church. The American bishops explain it this way: "Because Catholics believe that the celebration of the Eucharist is a sign of the reality of the oneness of faith, life, and worship, members of those churches with whom we are not yet fully united are ordinarily not admitted to Holy Communion."

They add: "Eucharistic sharing in exceptional circumstances by other Christians requires permission according to the directives of the diocesan bishop and the provisions of canon law."

And they say: "We also welcome [to the Mass] those who do not share our faith in Jesus Christ. While we cannot admit them to Holy Communion, we ask them to offer their prayers for the peace and unity of the human family."

This can be an emotional issue for some people. It's not intended to be exclusionary but a call to commitment and conversion.

Can a Catholic take the bread and wine at a Protestant service?
No. That kind of "reciprocity" is possible only with those churches that have preserved the substance of the Eucharist, the sacrament of orders, and apostolic succession.

Like the Orthodox Churches?
No. Within the churches commonly called "the East" are both Catholic and Orthodox. Catholic churches are those in union with the Roman Catholic Church; the Orthodox churches are separate from Rome and have their own patriarch. A Catholic may receive the sacraments in Catholic Churches of the Eastern rite. They may receive the Eucharist, penance, and anointing of the sick from priests of Orthodox churches only if they have

genuine spiritual need and seek spiritual benefit, and access to a Catholic priest is impossible.

In the latter case, the policy of reciprocity is based on the fact that the separated Eastern churches have apostolic succession through their bishops, valid priests, and sacramental beliefs and practices in accord with those of the Catholic Church.

If the Eucharist is offered under both bread and wine, do I have to receive both?
No, you can receive under bread alone.

Can I receive Communion more than once a day?
If you've already received Communion, you may receive it one more time that day during a eucharistic celebration in which you are participating. (In a sense of misguided devotion, you couldn't just blitz from parish Mass to parish Mass, dash in, receive Communion, and dash out.)

A person who has received once or even twice during a day but is in danger of death is urged to receive again as viaticum.

What's viaticum?
It's Latin for "provisions for the journey." This is the term used for Communion given to a person in danger of death.

Am I supposed to receive Communion on my tongue or in my hand?
The choice is yours.

I've heard the fancy display receptacle used to hold a big host called a "monster." Is that right?
It's a "monstrance." Both words have the same Latin root.

So the Eucharist is supposed to scare people?
No, not at all. *Monstrum* was used to mean a sign or wonder as well as an ogre. *Monstrance* is like "demonstrate," not "monster."

What about a "pixie"? For taking Communion to someone who's homebound or in the hospital?
Monsters and pixies, hmm. That little container is a "pyx," coming from the Latin for a powder or cosmetic box (like today's "compact"). While it may be tempting to connect pixie and pyx, the origin of the word for a little elf is unknown.

Why are there tabernacles, and where should they be in a church building?
The consecrated host needs to be kept in a safe place. Ideally a tabernacle is in a separate chapel suitable for private devotions (such as the Chapel of the Sacrament at St. Peter's Basilica in Rome). The General Instruction

of the Roman Missal states "every encouragement should be given to the practice of Eucharistic reservation in a chapel suited to the faithful's private adoration and prayer" (276). If that's not possible, then a side altar or other appropriately adorned place can be used.

Keep Holy the Lord's Day

When Christians speak of the "Sabbath," they mean the first day of the week. When Jews (and a few Christian groups) use that term, they mean the last.

It could be argued the Jews are right because, as told in the story of creation in Genesis, it was on the seventh day that God rested. In his commandment "Remember to keep holy the Lord's Day," he commanded his chosen people to do the same.

In Old Testament times the Sabbath was a weekly setting aside of everyday chores not only for the Israelites but for their slaves and animals, too. (The slaves were given the day off as a tip of the hat—a way of remembering—that when the Hebrews were in Egypt, they, too, were slaves.) Even the Hebrew word for that day has its roots in "rest."

The development of the relationship between the Sabbath and religious observances in the local synagogue showed that those observances didn't depend on the temple in Jerusalem, that they could be practiced anywhere.

Why Sunday?

Many members of the early Church who were devout Jews as well as sincere followers of "the Way" attended Jewish ceremonies on Saturday and took part in "the breaking of the bread" in homes on Sunday, as that was the day on which Christ had risen from the dead (see CCC 2174). Some tried to impose this form of dual worship on non-Jews who were joining the Church. The result was the decision—the teaching—that it wasn't necessary to keep the Jewish observance (Col 2:16).

But even today the Church says it *is* necessary—good, right, important—for Catholics to "keep the Sabbath" by attending Mass on the first day of the week. Sunday Eucharist remains the foundation and the confirmation of all Christian practice. A person needs a serious reason for missing this serious obligation. Two examples of legitimate excuses the *Catechism* gives are illness and the care of infants. To deliberately skip—to simply blow it off—is to commit a grave sin.

It's *that* important. We each need it *that* much. It's *that* central, basic, vital to being a Catholic. Paying attention to keeping the Lord's Day holy benefits us: "The sabbath was made for man, not man for the sabbath" (Mk 2:27).

We have a need to stop and praise our heavenly Father. We need to be with, in that incredible and very particular way, his Son, who came to get us out of the mess humanity had made (and we continue to contribute to). We need to be open to the Love between them, the Spirit, who can blow through our lives with incredible gifts—gifts that come in mighty handy during the rest of the week.

We have a need to join with others and pray with them and

for them and have them do the same. We need to, as we say in the Confiteor, "ask the Blessed Virgin Mary, all the angels and saints, and you my brothers and sisters, to pray to the Lord our God for me."

A Day of Rest

But wait, there's more! Sometimes we focus so much on "attending Mass" that we forget the other part of what is supposed to be our "Sabbath lifestyle." This day is a two-fer. We're also to "keep" it by making it a day of rest. Sometimes that part is tougher. Yes, we can get to Mass, but then we get into catching up on housework, yard work, "work" work; checking e-mails or slogging through some paperwork to ease the Monday morning crunch. And on and on.

There's truth to the observation "I have to get back to work to get some rest."

And there's truth to the fact that human beings, from the time of stone tablets to the time of cell phones, need a day of rest. God didn't give us the third commandment because he needs to be worshiped or for some reason needs to have us take time for rest and spend time with loved ones. Because he made us, he knows *we* need those things.

We have a need to set aside everyday cares and concerns, to call "time out" or "king's X." Keeping the Sabbath holy is God's ringing of the recess bell. It's time to go out and play.

The Code of Canon Law puts it this way: "On Sundays and other holy days of obligation the faithful are bound ... to abstain from those labors and business concerns which impede the worship to be rendered to God, the joy which is proper to the Lord's Day, or the proper relaxation of mind and body" (can. 1247).

That obligation isn't meant to add to our burdens but to lighten them, by giving us what is really not just a terrific but a truly divine excuse to take the day off. We have a reason solidly based on our religious belief. We have a commandment from God that says, "Enjoy!"

It's *good* to be Catholic.

That "institutionalizing" of the Sabbath, as the bishops noted in their Vatican II "Pastoral Constitution on the Church in the Modern World," helps all of us "to be allowed sufficient rest and leisure to cultivate [our] family, cultural, social, and religious lives" ("Pastoral Constitution on the Church in the Modern World," 67, 3).

But, the *Catechism* cautions, family needs or important social service can legitimately excuse us from the obligation of Sunday rest. Finding that proper balance—not coming up with lame excuses on either side—is to rely on the Holy Spirit's gift of wisdom.

We need our Sundays because our minds and bodies need that break. Even as science—from athletic trainers to psychological researchers—continues to "discover" just how true that is, and as the Church continues to preach it, the speed of our lives is ratcheted up yet another notch.

And that speed will increase again and again and again, if we let that happen. We do, after all, still have free will. We still can choose to keep the Sabbath "holy," setting it aside not as the first day of the week (getting a jump-start on this week's to-do list) but as the "eighth day."

Like the early Church, we celebrate on this day because it's the dawn of the new creation. The "eighth day" is our Sabbath because Christians are an "Easter people." We are getting a jump-start on heaven.

SIX

Reconciliation: Love Means Being Able to Say You're Sorry

Fully initiated into the Catholic Church, you still aren't perfect. Baptized and confirmed and a frequent recipient of the Eucharist, you still manage to—there's just no other word for it—sin.

Don't get defensive. You've got a *lot* of company. All human beings, except for Jesus and his mother Mary, have sinned. All of us continue to sin.

That, of course, includes Catholics, who manage to sin in ways both petty and profound. So the dilemma the early Church faced was what to do with people like you, not because there were people like you but because *they* were people like you. We *all* are people like you.

This chapter and the next will focus on the healing sacraments: reconciliation and the anointing of the sick. Through them Jesus offers you the same words and the same touch he extended to people during his public ministry. Beaten down and broken by sin, they were forgiven. Crippled, blind, deaf, mute, bleeding, diseased, dying, and even dead, they were restored to health.

Exactly who were healed? Those who came to Jesus and those whom others helped come to Jesus. And while the crowds rightly marveled at the physical recovery, Jesus pointedly asked,

"Which is easier, to say, 'Your sins are forgiven,' or to say, 'Rise and walk'?" (Mt 9:5).

Fashion Craze

In our own time "sin" can seem like an archaic, quaint, and certainly outdated concept. The ideas of fault, blame, personal responsibility, and the consequences of choices are less than fashionable. They're not popular ideas, and they never have been.

Sinning, on the other hand, is a perennial favorite. Sinning is that string of pearls or navy blue blazer that never goes out of style. That's why the Ten Commandments still "work." It's why they still annoy us.

We recognize their basic truth because—devout believer, atheist, or agnostic—we recognize basic morality. It isn't that every religion has that built-in "compass"; it's that *every human does*, every sinner. In recent times we may have gotten better at muddying the waters and pointing fingers. We may lean more heavily now on accusing others of being "judgmental" and depend more on "You can't tell me what's right for me, and if you have a problem with what I'm doing, then you're the one with the problem." But we know. Unless our conscience is severely damaged or has a basic defect, we know. Even if that conscience isn't highly honed and well informed and educated, we know.

There is right. There is wrong.

Yeah, but ... "Yeah, but ..." nothing. Yes, it might be lovely if there were no absolute right and wrong and so we could argue any position and defend that position and love that position. But we know.

We know because it's part of our basic makeup. It's how we're built. If we don't like it, we need to speak to the Builder. But then, it's the Builder who gave us the Ten Commandments. And, yes, as a matter of fact, they *were* carved in stone.

'Cause Mom Says

We humans don't like those two tablets because they tell us things we already know but don't want to hear. So we have— it could be said—beaten them into dust. That doesn't change who we are or what they are. That doesn't change Who gave them to us and why.

The *why* is important. The *why* is easily overlooked and conveniently ignored. And without the *why*, that list has all the appeal of a mom telling her five-year-old, "Don't leave the front yard, and pick up your toys." Do this. Don't do that. Do this. Don't do that.

OK, here's the problem with *that:* First of all, as the five-year-old, it seems to us Mommy said that and then went back in the house. Pick up the toys? Maybe later, maybe not. Don't leave the front yard? There's no fence. There's no physical impediment to our putting one toe over the line, with a quick glance back at the window. Nothing. Ha!

So we venture out, and since we aren't venturing far or for a long time, and since others are venturing much farther and longer, we therefore conclude:

1. We aren't so bad.
2. Others are much worse.
3. The rule was bogus.

Mom just made the rule up for no reason we can think of. And with God and us, we can even slide into the equivalent of "and Mom doesn't even exist." Or if she does, she's in watching TV and doesn't really care what we're up to. Or maybe Mom has died. Now, that last possibility should cause enormous grief and fear, but for a Roamin' Kid (or a Roman Catholic), it can be interpreted as "No more rules! All right! Free at last."

But what kind of freedom is that?

The Ten Commandments are all about freedom—not about restricting it but taking advantage of it. With the Ten Commandments we can use freedom to our advantage.

Yahweh Doesn't Double-Cross

Let's consider Yahweh for a moment. Let's assume that, being all-wise and all-loving, he's not going to shaft his chosen people. He saved them by getting them over to Egypt when famine was wiping out folks in their own land. He saved them by getting them out of Egypt when politics had shifted and they had become slaves. He saved them during their time in the desert with the basics of meat, bread, and water.

And at that point, for some reason, he was going to hand them something, force them to do something or avoid doing something, that was going to make their lives miserable? He was going to turn the chosen people into slaves of his rules?

That doesn't make sense. That can't be the *why* behind the Ten Commandments. So what is?

The Ten Commandments have to be based on wisdom and love; it can't be any other way. Consider the source: God. Consider the place: the harsh and even deadly desert. Consider the time: on the run from Pharaoh.

The commandments have to be good for the chosen people, and they have to be good for us. But how can that be so? Doesn't freedom mean we can do whatever we want?

Yes, and the commandments don't take away that ability to choose. As long as we're on earth, we have free will. This, too, is a gift from God. Simply put, the Ten Commandments are the instructions that come with the gift. So are the Beatitudes, the Gospels, all Scripture, the teachings of the Church.

Those instructions don't force us to use something in a particular way. We are perfectly free to assemble that bicycle any way we want, to hook up that DVD, to bolt together that propane barbecue. If we choose to do it our way or don't pay attention to how we're assembling it, the bike, the player, the grill, may work just fine. Or it may sort of work. Or it may not work at all. It may fall apart as we're riding it, fry our other electronic toys, blow up in our face.

Ditto with our lives. "I made you. Here's the best way for you to live—the one that will make you happiest, the one for which you were made. Now you choose. Get to work."

We have to "get to work" because we are each a work in progress. We play a hand in our own creation. We have the ability, through free will and God's grace, to become the person God created us to be—or more accurately, the one he gave us the potential to be. We have all the parts. Everything we need is right there or will be right there when we need it. Each and every one of us can become saints.

We're in This Together

Making us saints is what the commandments are all about. That's the *why*. Saints aren't boxed in by do's and don'ts. They never give up their freedom; they use it incredibly wisely. They understand not only the relationship between Creator and created one but among all created ones. They know we aren't just individuals, but made in the image and likeness of God, in imitation of the Trinity, we're called to live in relationships.

The Ten Commandments could be subtitled "How to Live in Relationships" *(Go to "The Decalogue Isn't an Olympic Event,"* p. 110). The first three are "us and God." The next seven are "us and us." Sin isn't breaking some arbitrary rule. (Here's the property line at the front of the house. Do not cross it.) It's breaking—damaging, chipping away at—a relationship.

The analogy of the mother and her five-year-old is a childish one. But typically, we learned about the commandments when we were children, and so any explanation was childish. It was what we could understand. The problem arises when, as our ability to understand increases, we don't replace whatever childish explanation we learned with a more mature one.

Even as we knew right from wrong and chose wrong, we failed to recognize the consequences of those actions *as we experienced those consequences.* We damaged our relationship with God and others. We damaged our relationship with *ourselves* (we with us). When we sin, we become less than we were created to be. Just as we play a part in "creating" ourselves, we can begin to destroy ourselves. It's our choice.

The sacrament of reconciliation is about restoring relationships. On the human level it involves admitting our faults and taking responsibility for what we've done, correcting those things. On the spiritual level it involves taking those failings to God in an act of trust—trusting in his mercy, trusting in his healing.

This sacrament is really a tremendous gift to us because it reconciles us to God, it reconciles us to the Church, it restores the dignity we were created to have within ourselves, and it gives us the grace of conversion. This is the grace of turning away from sin and back to love, God's life in us. As with every sacrament, we receive grace to change things in our hearts and in our lives.

Why Do We Need a Priest to Talk to God?

The *how* of this sacrament fascinates non-Catholics. The "confessional scene" remains a Hollywood favorite, and the "confessional seal" a great plot device.

The role of the priest—in real life, not the movies—is unique. He represents the Church and has the power to reconcile us to it. And he is allowed to be the instrument of God, to represent God and reconcile us to God.

How that is done—how the sacrament is celebrated—has varied a lot over the centuries. In the early Church reconciliation for someone who had committed a grave sin (such as idolatry, murder, or adultery) involved rigorous discipline. A person might have to perform public penance *for years* before receiving reconciliation. In some instances and places a person was admitted only one time to this "order of penitents."

It wasn't until the seventh century that Irish missionaries, taking their cue from Eastern monastic tradition, took the practice of "private" penance to continental Europe. That meant that public and prolonged completion of penitential works wasn't required before a person was reconciled with the Church. From then on, the sacrament was performed in secret between the penitent and priest.

The development of this practice led to repetition of the sacrament, and that led to going to confession regularly and frequently. The forgiveness of not just grave sins but venial sins was integrated into one sacramental celebration.

Even as that development evolved over the centuries, the same basic structure was there. There are two essential elements. The first, for anyone who undergoes this kind of conversion through the action of the Holy Spirit, is contrition, confession, and satisfaction (that is, the "penance"). The second is God's action through the intervention of the Church.

The Church, through its bishops and priests, forgives sin in the name of Christ and determines the manner of satisfaction. And the Church prays for the sinner and does penance with him or her. That's how the person is healed and reestablished in the Church community.

The formula of absolution used in the Latin Church shows those elements:

God, the Father of mercies,
through the death and resurrection of his Son,
has reconciled the world to himself
and sent the Holy Spirit among us
for the forgiveness of sins;
through the ministry of the Church
may God grant you pardon and peace,
and I absolve you from your sins
in the name of the Father, and of the Son,
and of the Holy Spirit.

To Hear Those Words

What does it take to hear those wonderful words, to receive the healing grace of this sacrament?

Reconciliation can be celebrated communally or individually. "Communally" doesn't mean publicly confessing one's sins. During a communal celebration there can be a reading from Scripture, a homily, and an examination of conscience conducted in common, but the person confesses his or her sins privately to the priest. That may be followed by a communal request for forgiveness, the Our Father, and a prayer of thanksgiving.

On rare occasions, if the number of people requesting confession is overwhelming, a general absolution is allowed. In that case, for the absolution to be valid, the person must have the intention of individually confessing grave sins.

Why is general absolution the exception? Because one-on-one is how Christ forgave. Again, it's how he gave us this sacrament. During his public ministry, and now, he addresses each person, saying, "Your sins are forgiven."

Whether celebrated communally or individually, reconciliation—like all the sacraments—is a liturgical action and so, in that sense, is always both ecclesial and public. And either way, the fundamental parts remain the same: contrition, confession, penance, and absolution.

Absolution: those wonderful words! that life-giving grace! Let's talk about the way we get there.

Contrition

At the Council of Trent the bishops wrote that contrition is "sorrow of the soul and detestation for the sin committed, together with the resolution not to sin again." When it's made from a love of God, it's called "perfect." Perfect contrition forgives venial sins and mortal also, if it includes the firm resolution to receive the sacrament of reconciliation as soon as possible.

"Imperfect" contrition is also a gift from God, a nudge from the Holy Spirit. But it's based on how "ugly" the sin is (we're mortified we could do such a thing) or on the fear of eternal damnation or other punishment. It can start the process that's completed by sacramental absolution, but by itself, imperfect contrition can't obtain the forgiveness of serious sins. It can help lead a person to the sacrament.

Confession

After a diligent examination of conscience, a person tells the priest his or her sins. All mortal sins must be confessed.

Church law says that "after having attained the age of

discretion, each of the faithful is bound by an obligation faithfully to confess serious sins at least once a year." And if a person is aware of having committed a mortal sin, he's not to receive Holy Communion—even if he experiences deep contrition—without having first received sacramental absolution. (The exception is if he has a grave reason for receiving the Eucharist and there's no possibility of going to confession.) Children are to go to confession before receiving First Holy Communion.

The confessing of "everyday faults"—venial sins—isn't necessary, but the Church highly recommends it. Regular confession of these faults helps a person form a conscience, fight against sinful tendencies, receive Christ's healing, and move forward in the life of the Spirit.

("Venial" means "pardonable." When talking about reconciliation, it refers to the fact that these sins can be forgiven without the sacrament. "Mortal" are grave or "deadly" sins. They cause so much damage, we are so wounded by them, that the sacrament of reconciliation is necessary.)

By more frequently receiving God's gift of mercy through this sacrament, we're led to be more merciful ourselves. In St. Augustine's words: "Whoever confesses his sins ... is already working with God.... The beginning of good works is the confession of evil works."

Penance

Another name for this is *satisfaction*. Sins have to do with relationships, and many are a matter of wronging a neighbor. We're called on to repair that damage to the extent that we can (to return stolen goods, for example, or to set the record straight if we've maliciously gossiped). That's justice.

But a sin also hurts us as well as our relationships with God and others. And while absolution takes away the sin, it doesn't automatically fix all the problems caused by our sinning. Our saying "Sorry," and truly meaning it, doesn't set everything right. To be restored to "full spiritual health," we need to *do* something more to make amends. We have to "make satisfaction for" or "expiate" our sins.

That's what the task, the penance, the priest gives is all about. The confessor considers our situation and wants us to be restored to full health. That's why a penance corresponds as far as possible to the seriousness and nature of the sin committed.

A penance can be a prayer, an offering, works of mercy, service to others, voluntary self-denial, sacrifices, and to quote the *Catechism*, "above all the patient acceptance of the cross we must bear" (CCC 1460).

A penance "configures" us to Christ, who alone made satisfaction for our sins once and for all. It allows us "to become coheirs with the risen Christ, 'provided we suffer with him'" (CCC 1460; Rom 8:17; Rom 3:25; 1 Jn 2:1-2; see Council of Trent [1551]: DS 1690).

Sorrow for sins, confession, and reparation with penance are the *matter* of this sacrament. Absolution is the *form*.

It's All About Healing

Through Christ's suffering, because of Christ's suffering, we can be healed. As the *Catechism* points out, just from a human standpoint it's therapeutic to seriously examine one's words, thoughts, and deeds—in the words of the Confiteor, "what I have done and what I have failed to do." To disclose those faults, to confess, frees us and helps us reconcile with others.

Looking honestly at our sins and taking responsibility for them opens us again to God and to the communion of the Church, to make a new future possible. Even so, this sacrament isn't easy. It's hard to tell ourselves what we've done. It's harder still to tell someone else, even a priest who acts *in persona Christi.*

There's temptation, even when approaching Christ in the sacrament, to gloss over one or two sins, to skip an area, to fail to mention a serious act. Even as we step forward to admit we're less than perfect, we want to hedge our confession and not be *that* imperfect.

After all, we may reason, if every sin is forgiven—if we're going to be receiving a blanket amnesty, a full pardon—then it isn't really necessary to say everything. But the Church says serious sins (grave sins, mortal sins) that we're aware of must be confessed. And while that isn't required for the pardon of venial sins, it would be foolish to remain silent, to cover up.

What we feel is nothing new. The *Catechism*, written at the end of the twentieth century, quotes the Council of Trent, which met in the sixteenth, nodding toward the writings of St. Jerome, who died in the early fifth: "For if a sick person is too ashamed to show his wound to the doctor, the medicine cannot heal what it does not know."

We don't go to confession because God wants us to suffer some sort of "payback" for breaking one of his commandments. We go because we're already suffering. Sin hurts us and our relationships, both with God and with others, especially those whom we love and those who love us.

Confession "hurts" because admitting faults hurts. Reconciliation "hurts" because our faults have some consequences that aren't magically, or even mystically, resolved. It takes work to untangle that web we've woven, the one that has limited us—blocked our ability to freely choose goodness and happiness—and has caused others harm, too.

In his 1984 apostolic exhortation "Reconciliation and Penance," Pope John Paul II explained it this way:

> It must be recalled that ... this reconciliation with God leads, as it were, to other reconciliations, which repair the other breaches caused by sin. The forgiven penitent is reconciled with himself in his inmost being, where he regains his innermost truth. He is reconciled with his brethren whom he has in some way offended and wounded. He is reconciled with the Church. He is reconciled with all creation.

The Decalogue Isn't an Olympic Event

The Decalogue—from the Greek for "ten words"—is another name for the Ten Commandments. We get that list from two Old Testament passages: Exodus 20:1-17 and Deuteronomy 5:6-21.

In the traditional Catholic numbering, based on Deuteronomy, they are

1. I, the Lord, am your God. You shall not have other gods beside me. You shall not carve idols.
2. You shall not take the name of the Lord, your God, in vain.
3. Take care to keep holy the Sabbath day.
4. Honor your father and your mother.
5. You shall not kill.
6. You shall not commit adultery.
7. You shall not steal.
8. You shall not bear false witness against your neighbor.
9. You shall not covet your neighbor's wife.
10. You shall not covet your neighbor's house or field, nor his male or female slave, nor his ox or ass, nor anything that belongs to him.

In the Protestant tradition the first commandment is split into two commandments, and the ninth and tenth are combined into one.

The mention of slavery is jarring to us, but at that time and place slavery was commonly accepted. What Yahweh had to teach the people, what Christ would teach, and how those teachings would develop over time within the Church was still unfolding.

The Decalogue should be seen as the minimum. It's bare bones. The list was well known in Jesus' time, and one fellow (Luke says "a lawyer") who came to him was looking for that minimum requirement. Jesus abridged but didn't minimize: "You shall love the Lord your God with all your heart, and with all your soul, and with all your mind. This is the greatest and first commandment. And a second is like it. You shall love your neighbor as yourself. On these two commandments depend all the Law and the prophets" (Mt 22:37-40; Mk 12:28-34; Lk 10:25-28; Dt 6:5; Lv 19:18).

In Luke's account the lawyer pressed the issue, looking for a loophole: "Who's my neighbor?" Jesus answered with the parable of the Good Samaritan.

Q & A: Why Not Go Directly to God?

Why does a Catholic go to a priest to confess his sins? Why not go directly to God?
The priest is an instrument of God. If you asked a Christian, Catholic or Protestant, "Who baptized you?" the typical answer would be "My pastor."

"What happened in that baptism?"

"My sins were washed away."

Right. God uses human instruments to work on his behalf.

What's the scriptural basis for this?
The foundation for both the sacrament and the priest's role in it is Matthew 16. Jesus asked his disciples, "Who do you say I am?" and Peter answered, "The Messiah. The Son of the living God." Jesus replied:

Blessed are you, Simon Bar-Jona!... And I tell you, you are Peter, and on this rock I will build my church, and the powers of death shall not prevail against it. I will give you the keys of the king-dom of heaven, and whatever you bind on earth shall be bound in heaven, and whatever you loose on earth shall be loosed in heaven.

MATTHEW 16:17-19

What's this sacrament like from the priest's point of view?
Despite some stereotypical movie scenes and the tall tales from some who "grew up Catholic," the priest is not out to "get" a penitent. To hear another's confession, to be God's instrument in this sacrament, is a humbling experience. The priest certainly knows that he, too, is far from perfect, and here is someone coming to God—reconciling himself to God, to the Church, to others, to himself—through the priest.

How does the Church see the priest?
The images the *Catechism* uses to describe this role are helpful. As a confessor, he is fulfilling his ministry of Good Shepherd, seeking the lost sheep; of Good Samaritan, binding up wounds; of the father waiting for the Prodigal Son and welcoming him with open arms; of the just and impartial judge, whose judgment is both fair and merciful. The priest is both the sign and the instrument of God's merciful love for the sinner. Far from being the "master" of God's forgiveness, he is its servant.

SEVEN

Anointing of the Sick: Christ's Healing Touch

In the not-too-distant past the call to the priest was made just before the call to the undertaker. If Father entered a sick person's room, the patient knew he or she was at death's door. "Extreme unction" was limited to extreme cases.

There's still a remnant of the feeling that getting Father involved is throwing in the towel. But that's not true. Anointing of the sick isn't giving up; it's giving over. It's handing to God all the fears, the pain, the anxieties, and the sins and receiving his grace in return.

It is the healing touch of Jesus.

Just as the Church calls us to help those who are hungry or homeless, we're called to do the same for those who are sick and suffering. At the heart of that is the unique sacramental call to help people find meaning and dignity in their illness and pain and unite those personal trials with the cross. *(Go to "John Paul II on Suffering," p. 121.)*

While sickness and suffering are a part of every life, we have a choice of how we will live with them even when they end in our death. As the *Catechism* points out, illness and suffering can make us feel powerless and limited. They can give us a glimpse of our own mortality. They can foster anguish, self-absorption, and sometimes despair and a revolt against God.

Yet sickness and suffering can also promote maturity, helping us figure out what really matters in our life. It's not unusual that an illness or a life-threatening accident sparks a search for God and a return to him.

This sacrament kindles that flame.

Jesus as Healer

The Gospels are filled with stories of Jesus' healing countless people. The evangelists are careful to note that he not only cured individuals of their illness or infirmity but also forgave their sins. Again, there is that link to the other healing sacrament: reconciliation.

Jesus came to offer complete healing, body and soul. His preferential love for the sick was so strong that he identified himself with them: "I was sick and you visited me" (Mt 25:36), and, "He took our infirmities and bore our diseases" (Mt 8:17; see Is 53:4).

Those healings announced one that was even more radical: the victory over sin and death. We will all suffer, we will all die, but suffering and death—ultimately—do not win. On his cross Jesus took upon himself "the whole weight of evil" and took away the sin of the world, of which illness is a consequence (again, going back to original sin and baptism).

That's why, by his passion and death, Jesus has given new meaning to all suffering. It can "configure us to him and unite us with his redemptive Passion" (CCC 1505). Christ commands those who would follow him to take up their own cross (see Mt 10:38).

By following him we can get a new outlook on our own

illness, suffering, and pain but also on all illness, suffering, and pain. We can get a new outlook on those who are sick and suffering. We can get a truly Christian—a Christlike—outlook as we imitate the disciples he sent out during his public ministry. They preached repentance, "cast out many demons, and anointed with oil many that were sick and healed them" (Mk 6:12-13).

Jesus' command to "heal the sick" (Mt 10:8) is one that applies to the Church of the twenty-first century as well as the first. That's why it strives to carry it out. Why it takes care of the sick as well as accompanying them with prayers and intercessions (see CCC 1509).

The Church believes in the life-giving presence of Christ, who remains the physician of souls and bodies. It's through the sacraments—and in a special way in the Eucharist—that this presence is particularly active. It is always Christ who heals, and that healing can happen on spiritual, emotional, and physical levels.

In this sacrament the Church guarantees there will be healing. (Again, a sacrament is "efficacious": It does what it says it will do.) There is spiritual healing in the forgiveness of sins. There is emotional healing because an increase of trust, of faith, can free a person from anxiety. Then, too, sometimes that emotional healing involves a relationship that has been bruised or broken. Not infrequently physical healing takes place, but that is not to say that there is *always* a physical cure or that death is *always* delayed.

Among the seven sacraments, the Church says, it's the anointing of the sick that is especially intended to strengthen those who are being tried by illness. "Is any among you sick? Let him call for the elders of the church, and let them pray over him, anointing him with oil in the name of the Lord; and the prayer of faith will save the sick man, and the Lord will raise him up; and if he has committed sins, he will be forgiven" (Jas 5:14-15).

Knocking at Death's Door

While that liturgical tradition continued in both the East and the West, over the centuries the anointing of the sick was conferred more and more exclusively on those at the point of death. That's how this sacrament received the name "extreme unction" ("extreme"—at the very end; "unction"—an anointing with oil). Even so, the bishops at the Council of Trent noted, "The liturgy has never failed to beg the Lord that the sick person may recover his health if it would be conducive to his salvation" (DS 1696).

Four centuries later the bishops of Vatican II wrote: "[The anointing of the sick] is not a sacrament for those only who are at the point of death. Hence, as soon as anyone of the faithful begins to be in danger of death from sickness or old age, the fitting time for him to receive this sacrament has certainly already arrived" ("Constitution on the Sacred Liturgy," 73).

When teaching about this sacrament today, the Church also stresses

- If the sick person recovers his health, he can in the case of another grave illness receive it again.
- If during the same illness his condition becomes more serious, the sacrament can be repeated.

- It's fitting to receive the anointing just prior to a serious operation, and the same holds true for the elderly person whose frailty becomes more pronounced.
- Someone who is unconscious can be anointed if it's believed he would have desired the sacrament.

At Home or in a Hospital

There may be more uncertainty these days among family members about when to call the priest or even whether to make that call. As to the whether, yes. God's grace, Jesus' touch, awaits. As to the when, anytime—but it's never too soon to talk to the priest about it.

The Church tells pastors to encourage the faithful to ask for the sacrament. The persons who are going to receive it should prepare themselves "with good dispositions, assisted by their pastor and the whole ecclesial community, which is invited to surround the sick in a special way through their prayers and fraternal attention" (CCC 1516). *(Go to "Q & A: How Do We Prepare for the Sacrament?" p. 123.)*

Only priests and bishops administer this sacrament. Whether celebrated with only the priest and the patient or with others, the anointing of the sick is a liturgical event. It's communal whether it takes place in a family home, hospital, nursing home, or church; whether it's only one sick person or a whole group.

The *Catechism* explains that it is "very fitting" to celebrate the anointing of the sick within the eucharistic celebration. If possible, it can be preceded by the sacrament of reconciliation and followed by the Eucharist. "As the sacrament of Christ's Passover the Eucharist should always be the last sacrament of the earthly journey, the 'viaticum' for 'passing over' to eternal life" (CCC 1517).

Just as baptism, confirmation, and Eucharist can be called the sacraments of initiation, so reconciliation, the anointing of the sick, and the Eucharist as viaticum "constitute at the end of Christian life 'the sacraments that prepare for our heavenly homeland' or the sacraments that complete the earthly pilgrimage" (CCC 1525). In times past they were termed "the last rites." That's still a common expression.

The Rite of Anointing

The actual rite is simple. There are the prayers of the Church, the laying on of hands, and the anointing with oil. (The oil, as mentioned in chapter three, typically is blessed by the bishop during Holy Week.) In the Roman rite the forehead and hands are anointed. In the Eastern rite, other parts of the body are, too.

The *matter* for this sacrament is the anointing with oil. The *form* is: "Through this holy anointing and his most loving mercy, may the Lord assist you by the grace of the Holy Spirit so that, when you have been freed from your sins, he may save you and in his goodness raise you up."

Again, the purpose of this sacrament is healing, but that doesn't always mean a return to robust health. Jesus' healing touch may mean a longer life. It may mean a more "beautiful death" because—released from fear or anxiety—one is prepared to see God face-to-face. It may mean—with the healing of the soul—that he or she will enjoy new life in heaven.

John Paul II on Suffering

In confronting sickness and death, Pope John Paul II's apostolic letter on suffering offers us wisdom and comfort:

> Down through the centuries and generations it has been seen that *in suffering there is concealed* a particular *power that draws a person interiorly close to Christ,* a special grace.
>
> To this grace many saints, such as Saint Francis of Assisi, Saint Ignatius of Loyola and others, owe their profound conversion. A result of such a conversion is not only that the individual discovers the salvific meaning of suffering but above all that he becomes a completely new person. He discovers a new dimension, as it were, of *his entire life and vocation.*
>
> This discovery is a particular confirmation of the spiritual greatness which in man surpasses the body in a way that is completely beyond compare. When this body is gravely ill, totally incapacitated, and the person is almost incapable of living and acting, all the more do interior *maturity and spiritual greatness* become evident, constituting a touching lesson to those who are healthy and normal.
>
> This interior maturity and spiritual greatness in suffering are certainly the *result* of a particular *conversion* and cooperation with the grace of the Crucified Redeemer. It is he himself who acts at the heart of human sufferings

through his Spirit of truth, through the consoling Spirit. It is he who transforms, in a certain sense, the very substance of the spiritual life, indicating for the person who suffers a place close to himself. *It is he*—as the interior Master and Guide—*who reveals* to the suffering brother and sister this *wonderful interchange,* situated at the very heart of the mystery of the Redemption.

Suffering is, in itself, an experience of evil. But Christ has made suffering the firmest basis of the definitive good, namely the good of eternal salvation. By his suffering on the Cross, Christ reached the very roots of evil, of sin and death. He conquered the author of evil, Satan, and his permanent rebellion against the Creator. To the suffering brother or sister Christ *discloses* and gradually reveals *the horizons of the Kingdom of God:* the horizons of a world converted to the Creator, of a world free from sin, a world being built on the saving power of love. And slowly but effectively, Christ leads into this world, into this Kingdom of the Father, suffering man, in a certain sense through the very heart of his suffering.

For suffering cannot be *transformed* and changed by a grace from outside, but *from within.* And Christ through his own salvific suffering is very much present in every human suffering and can act from within that suffering by the powers of his Spirit of truth, his consoling Spirit.

Pope John Paul II, Salvific Doloris, 1984

Q & A: How Do We Prepare for the Sacrament?

What do we do before the priest comes for the anointing?
The most important preparation is spiritual: praying for and with the one who will receive the anointing.

What do we need to have on hand?
Nothing. The priest brings the oil with him.

What about candles?
You don't need to have any candles.

What about one of those special crosses, a "sick call set"?
At one time many Catholic homes had a "sick call crucifix." Two small candles and a bottle for holy water were stored in the cross behind a removable front crucifix. The back could be set on a table to hold the crucifix upright, with slots for the candles on each side. These are nice to have but not necessary for the sacrament.

Is a funeral part of the "last rites"?
No. It's a liturgical celebration that can be held in the home, the church, or the cemetery. At each there's the greeting of the community, the liturgy of the Word, the Eucharist (when the celebration takes place in a church), and the farewell.

What's the "farewell"?

It's saying good-bye to the deceased and his final "commendation to God" by the Church. In the Byzantine tradition the "kiss of farewell" is expressed this way:

By this final greeting "we sing for his departure from this life and separation from us, but also because there is a communion and a reunion. For even dead, we are not at all separated from one another, because we all run the same course and we will find one another again in the same place. We shall never be separated, for we live in Christ, and now we are united with Christ as we go toward him ... we shall all be together in Christ."

EIGHT

Holy Orders: The Call to Serve

There's no such thing as a selfish or private sacrament. There's no "only God and me" sacrament. But in a unique way, holy orders and matrimony have to do with serving others. It's through service that each of them may contribute to the recipient's personal salvation—may help that person get to heaven.

It's also through holy orders and matrimony that those already consecrated by baptism and confirmation for the "common priesthood" of all Christians can receive particular consecrations. Those who are ordained are consecrated in Christ's name—quoting Vatican II's "Dogmatic Constitution on the Church"—"to feed the Church by the Word and grace of God." And those who marry in the Church—quoting the council's "Pastoral Constitution on the Church in the Modern World"—become "Christian spouses [who] are fortified and, as it were, consecrated for the duties and dignity of their state by a special sacrament." (48, 2)

All Christians Are "Priestly"

A distinction needs to be made between the "common priesthood" and the "ministerial priesthood."

Christ, the High Priest, made the Church "a kingdom, priests serving his God and Father" (Rv 1:6). The entire Christian community—the *ecclesia*, the gathering—is priestly. We each exercise our "baptismal priesthood" by our participation in Christ's mission as priest, prophet, and king. How we do that depends on our particular vocation, but it's through our baptism and confirmation that we are already "consecrated to be ... a holy priesthood" ("Dogmatic Constitution on the Church," 10, 1).

That's the "common priesthood." The "ministerial priesthood"—made up of those who have been ordained—exists to serve it. And it's through the ministerial priesthood that Christ unceasingly builds up and leads his Church. That's why it's "transmitted by its own sacrament, the sacrament of Holy Orders" (CCC 1547).

The authority Christ gave to his apostles is present within the ministerial priesthood today. Ordination confers the gift of the Holy Spirit for the exercise of "sacred power" that can come only from Christ himself through his Church. And ordination is a consecration because it's a setting apart and an investiture by Christ himself for his Church.

Just as the apostles didn't replace Jesus, couldn't replace Jesus, so too, with those who receive the sacrament of holy orders today. In the words of St. Thomas Aquinas, "Only Christ is the true priest, the others being only his ministers."

What "Orders" Really Means

In the Roman world of the early Church, the Latin word *ordo* commonly meant an established civil body, especially one that governed. A person became a member of an *ordo* through *ordinatio.* Neither word was used only by the Church, but the Church used both words.

Since that time there have been established bodies within the Church that Tradition, based in Scripture, has called *ordines* (the plural of *ordo*). The liturgy speaks of the *ordo episcoporum,* the *ordo presbyterium,* and the *ordo diaconorum.* (There have been others—the *ordo* of catechumens, for example.)

Within the Church the rite known as an *ordinatio* was a religious and liturgical act that was a consecration, a blessing, or a sacrament. Today we commonly use *ordination* only for the sacramental act that integrates men into the order of bishops, presbyters (priests), or deacons. This order goes beyond a simple election, designation, delegation, or institution by the community.

The Sacrament's "Jewish Roots"

As is so often the case in Christianity, the sacrament of holy orders shows the Church's Jewish roots. That's not to say that in the ancient world Israel was the only nation to have priests. The priesthood, generally hereditary and divided into a large number of classes with special functions, was common in many regions and cultures.

The Old Testament—the "Hebrew Scriptures" or "old covenant"—tells of God's making the chosen people "a kingdom of priests and a holy nation" (Ex 19:6; see Is 61:6). Within all the Israelites, Yahweh chose to set apart the tribe of Levi for liturgical services and said he himself would be the

Levites' inheritance (see Nm 1:48-53). Moses' brother Aaron and his sons were designated (Ex 28) and installed (Lv 8) as priests, with Aaron as the high priest.

There was a special rite of consecration at the beginning of the old covenant priesthood. Members were "appointed to act on behalf of men in relation to God, to offer gifts and sacrifice for sins" (Heb 5:1; see Ex 29:1-30; Lv 8).

This priesthood—even though it was instituted to proclaim the Word of God and restore harmony with Yahweh by sacrifices and prayers—didn't have the power to bring about salvation. Sacrifices had to be repeated, and the Levites were unable "to achieve a definite sanctification, which only the sacrifice of Christ would accomplish" (CCC 1540; see Heb 5:3; 7:27; 10:1-4). Even so, now in its liturgy the Church remembers those early priests and sees them as a prefiguring of the ordained ministry of the new covenant.

At the ordination of bishops, priests, or deacons, the sign of holy orders is the laying on of hands, the prayer, and the anointing with holy oil. In the Latin rite the Church expresses its Jewish roots in the prayers:

At the ordination of bishops: "From the beginning, you chose the descendants of Abraham to be your holy nation. You established rulers and priests, and did not leave your sanctuary without ministers to serve you."

At the ordination of priests: "You extended the spirit of Moses to seventy wise men.... You shared among the sons of Aaron the fullness of their father's power."

At the ordination of deacons: "As ministers of your tabernacle you chose the sons of Levi and gave them your blessing as their everlasting inheritance."

Bishops: Today's Apostles

While the three stages of holy orders include the ordination of bishops, priests, and deacons, "the fullness of the sacrament ... is conferred by episcopal consecration, that fullness, namely, which both in the liturgical tradition of the Church and the language of the Fathers of the Church [the early theologians] is called the high priesthood, the acme [summa] of the sacred ministry" ("Dogmatic Constitution on the Church," 21).

Being consecrated a bishop "confers, together with the office of sanctifying, the duty also of teaching and ruling.... In fact,... by the imposition of hands and through the words of the consecration, the grace of the Holy Spirit is given, and a sacred character is impressed in such wise that bishops, in an eminent and visible manner, take the place of Christ himself, teacher, shepherd, and priest, and act as his representatives" ("Dogmatic Constitution on the Church," 21).

"By virtue, therefore, of the Holy Spirit who has been given to them, bishops have been constituted true and authentic teachers of the faith and have been made pontiffs and pastors" (Vatican II, "Decree on the Pastoral Office of Bishops in the Church," 2).

(Every bishop is a "pontiff," a word that comes from the Latin for "bridge builder." In our own time, generally only the pope—the "supreme pontiff"—is referred to with that title.)

A bishop, successor to the apostles, has the power to administer all the sacraments, has jurisdiction of a diocese (a geographic area), and is a member of the "college of bishops." The character and the collegial nature of bishops were shown in the Church's early practice of having several bishops participate in the consecration of a new bishop.

Today the lawful ordination of a bishop requires a special intervention of the bishop of Rome—the pope—because he is the "supreme visible bond of the communion of the particular Churches in the one Church and the guarantor of their freedom" (CCC 1559).

So as Christ's "vicar"—from the Latin for "deputy"—each bishop has the pastoral care of a particular diocese entrusted to him; at the same time he shares a collegiality with all the bishops for the care of all dioceses. "Though each bishop is the lawful pastor only of the portion of the flock entrusted to his care, as a legitimate successor of the apostles he is, by divine institution and precept, responsible with the other bishops for the apostolic mission of the Church" (Pius XII, *Fidei donum*).

Priests: A Bishop's Coworkers

Every bishop has first been ordained a priest.

Simply put, priests are bishops' coworkers. They can administer the sacraments of baptism, Eucharist, reconciliation, marriage, anointing of the sick, and under limited circumstances, confirmation. They can't ordain.

Just as, typically, a bishop's jurisdiction is a diocese, a priest's is a parish.

Since the beginning of the Church, "the function of the bishops' ministry was handed over in a subordinate degree to priests so that they might be appointed in the order of priesthood and be coworkers of the episcopal order for the proper fulfillment of the apostolic mission that had been entrusted to it by Christ" (Vatican II, "Decree on the Ministry and Life of Priests," 1, 2).

Because of that relationship, priests share in the authority "by which Christ himself builds up and sanctifies and rules his Body" (CCC 1563). So "the priesthood of priests"—a term used to distinguish it from the common priesthood—is conferred by its own particular sacrament. Through that sacrament a man, by the anointing of the Holy Spirit, is signed with a special character and configured to Christ in such a way that he is able to act *in persona Christi:* in the person of Christ, the Head of the Church.

Even though a priest doesn't have the "supreme degree of the pontifical office," and even though he depends on a bishop in the exercise of his own proper power, he is associated with the bishop. He shares "in the universal dimensions of the mission that Christ entrusted to the apostles" (CCC 1565).

It's in the Eucharist—at Mass—that the priest exercises in a supreme degree his sacred office. At Mass priests "'acting in the person of Christ and proclaiming his mystery,... unite the votive offerings of the faithful to the sacrifice of Christ their head, and in the sacrifice of the Mass they make present again and apply, until the coming of the Lord, the unique sacrifice of the New Testament, that namely of Christ offering himself once for all a spotless victim to the Father.' From this unique sacrifice their whole priestly ministry draws its strength"

(CCC 1566; see "Decree on the Ministry and Life of Priests," 2).

Within the local assembly—the parish or faith community—the priest represents, in a certain sense, the bishop. Priests take on themselves the bishop's "duties and solicitude and in their daily toils discharge them" ("Dogmatic Constitution on the Church," 28).

A priest can exercise his ministry only in dependence on the bishop and in communion with him. The promise of obedience he makes to the bishop during the ordination rite and the kiss of peace he receives from the bishop at the end of that liturgy mean that the bishop can consider him a coworker, a son, a brother, and a friend. And the priest, in return, owes the bishop love and obedience.

There's also a relationship among all priests, who are bound together by "an intimate sacramental brotherhood" ("Decree on the Ministry and Life of Priests," 2, 8). In a special way they form one body within the diocese to which they are attached under their own bishop. That unity is expressed liturgically at an ordination when priests impose their hands on the "ordinand" after the bishop has. *(Go to "Q & A: Who Can Be a Priest?"* p. 136.)

Deacons: A Life of Service

Deacons—those in the "lower level of the hierarchy"—also receive the imposition of hands during their ordination. Then it's "not unto priesthood, but unto ministry" ("Dogmatic Constitution on the Church," 29). Only the bishop lays hands on the candidate, and that signifies the deacon's special attachment to the bishop in the task of his *diakonia*—his particular ministry of service.

A deacon can administer the sacrament of baptism and, under limited circumstances, preside over the celebration of marriage. His "jurisdiction" is works of charity. His role is service.

Just as with episcopal and priestly ordination, when a deacon receives holy orders there is an imprint (a character) that cannot be removed. It "configures" the man to Christ, who made himself the "deacon"—the servant—of all.

Among the duties of a deacon are to assist the bishop and priest in the celebration of the Eucharist, to distribute Communion, to assist at and bless marriages, to proclaim the Gospel and preach, to preside over funerals, and to dedicate himself to various ministries of charity.

As a step toward priestly ordination, a man is ordained a "transitional deacon." While the role of deacons is recorded in the Acts of the Apostles and has always been a part of the Churches of the East, in the Latin Church it was after Vatican II that the permanent diaconate was restored. It's seen "as a proper and permanent rank of the hierarchy" ("Dogmatic Constitution on the Church," 29).

The Church says it's both appropriate and useful that men who carry out the diaconal ministry, whether in the Church's liturgical and pastoral life or in its social and charitable works, should "be strengthened by the imposition of hands which has come down from the apostles." Through the sacramental grace of the diaconate, those who receive this order are "more closely bound to the altar and their ministry ... made more fruitful" (Vatican II, "Decree on the Church's Missionary Activity," 16).

When Pope Paul VI restored the permanent diaconate in the Roman rite, he specified that

- Qualified unmarried men twenty-five or older may be ordained. They can't marry after ordination.
- Qualified married men thirty-five or older may be ordained. The consent of the wife of the prospective deacon is required. A married deacon cannot remarry after the death of his spouse.
- Preparation for the diaconate includes a course of study and formation over a period of at least three years.
- Candidates who are not members of religious institutes must be affiliated with a diocese.
- Deacons practice their ministry under the direction of a bishop and with the priest with whom they will be associated.

In the not-too-distant past there were seven separate degrees of holy orders in the Western Church. That changed soon after Vatican II. (*Go to "Tonsure and the 'Minor' League,"* p. 1340.)

A Clerical Who's Who

Historically, a secular priest is one ordained for and associated with a diocese. A secular priest pledges obedience to the bishop and makes a promise of celibacy.

A "religious" or "order" priest belongs to a particular order or society, such as the Dominicans or Jesuits. Religious priests take vows of poverty, chastity, and obedience prior to ordination. (A religious brother would have taken the same vows.)

"Monsignor" is an honorary title given to some priests by the pope.

Within the ranks of bishops are the pope and cardinals. The pope is the bishop of Rome. He is elected by the college of cardinals. Cardinals are bishops who have been chosen by a pope to serve as his principal assistants and as advisors in the central administration of Church affairs. Collectively they form the "college."

Traditionally, it *is* possible to tell the players without a program because each has a distinctive cassock. The pope wears white, a tradition dating back to the sixteenth century pope Pius V, who, as white-habited Dominicans are quick to point out, was a member of their order. Cardinals are in red, bishops in purple, while monsignors may have purple piping on black. Priests, deacons, and seminarians are in basic black.

At an Ordination

An ordination isn't a secret ritual. Just the opposite. The faithful are encouraged to attend and to take part. That's why, ideally, it takes place on a Sunday at a cathedral. The proper liturgical setting is within the Mass.

The essential rite for the ordination of a bishop, priest, or deacon consists of the bishop's imposition of hands on the head of the man and the bishop's specific prayer for the outpouring of the Holy Spirit and his gifts proper to that ministry. There can be various additional rites, too. In the Latin Church the initial rites are

- the presentation and election of the ordinand
- instruction by the bishop
- examination of the candidate
- litany of the saints

After the essential rite for a bishop and priest there is an anointing with chrism. This is a sign of the special anointing of the Holy Spirit, who makes the ordinand's ministry bear fruit.

For a bishop there is the giving of the book of the Gospels, the ring, the miter (hat), and the crosier (staff). These are signs of his apostolic mission to proclaim the Word of God, of his fidelity to the Church (the bride of Christ), and of his office as shepherd of the Lord's flock.

For a priest there is the presentation of the chalice and paten, "the offering of the holy people" he's called to present to God.

For a deacon there is the giving of the book of the Gospels, symbolizing his mission to proclaim the gospel of Christ.

Q & A: Who Can Be a Priest?

Who can be a priest?
Only a baptized man validly receives ordination.

Why only a man?
The *Catechism* explains it this way:

The Lord Jesus chose men *(viri)* to form the college of the twelve apostles, and the apostles did the same when they chose collaborators to succeed them in their ministry. The college of bishops, with whom the priests are united in the priesthood, makes the college of the twelve an ever-present and ever-active reality until Christ's return. The Church recognizes herself to be bound by this choice made by the Lord himself. For this reason the ordination of women is not possible (CCC 1577; see Mk 3:14-19; Lk 6:12-16; 1 Tm 3:1-13; Ti 1:5-9).

What does "is not possible" mean?

As with all the sacraments, holy orders doesn't exist because the Church decided it would be a good idea. It was given to the Church by Christ. While some particulars have varied since Jesus instituted holy orders, at its core it exists today as he gave it to the Church. The Church doesn't have the authority to have it be otherwise. That's also true with the other six sacraments.

Who decides if a particular man will be ordained?

God and the Church. No man has the *right* to be ordained; it's God's call. If a man thinks he has that vocation, he submits his desire to the authority of the Church, which has the responsibility and right to call someone to receive orders. As with every grace, this sacrament can be received only as an unmerited gift. A man doesn't somehow "earn" ordination.

Why can't priests get married?
With the exception of permanent deacons, ordained ministers in the Latin Church are normally chosen "from among men of faith who live a celibate life and who intend to remain celibate 'for the sake of the kingdom of heaven'" (CCC 1579; Mt 19:12). Celibacy is a sign of the priest's life of service.

Aren't some priests married?
In the Eastern Churches married men are ordained priests and deacons. Only celibates are bishops. A single man who is ordained cannot then marry.

In the West all priests are normally celibate. In recent times there have been exceptions for married men who were ordained ministers in other denominations and who have become Roman Catholic.

Weren't the apostles married?
Some were. Historians say celibacy has been a part of the Church since at least the early fourth century and has been a requirement, in the West, since the eleventh.

What's an "ex-priest"?
It's the common term for priests who have had their faculties revoked and for priests who have been laicized. In either case, it's an inaccurate description. Once a man is ordained he is ordained forever. Just as in baptism and confirmation, there is that indelible mark or character. It would be equally inaccurate to call someone an

"ex-Christian," as if that person had somehow lost, given up, or had taken away the mark he or she received at baptism.

What does "had their faculties revoked" mean?

While ordination brings the power to act *in persona Christi,* the right to exercise that power is granted by a bishop. If there is a serious reason to do so, a bishop may rescind—take back—the faculties he has given a priest, and the priest can no longer legally celebrate the sacraments.

Can he do it "illegally"?

The Church has authority over the sacraments since they have been given to the Church by Christ. For a sacrament to be valid it must meet certain criteria. For instance, a validly ordained priest must say the Eucharistic prayer over bread and wine in order for transubstantiation to take place.

A sacrament can be valid (really happen) but also be illicit (illegal according to Church law). For example, if a priest leads a schismatic group outside the authority of the Church he may validly consecrate the Eucharist but the sacrament would be considered illicit.

It's the responsibility of every Catholic to stay in unity with the Church. All sacraments should be celebrated in a *valid* and *licit* form. A Catholic can presume that his or her parish priest and parish community are doing just that, unless the bishop has stated something to the contrary.

What does "defrocked" mean?
It's an older term for the rescinding of faculties. It's a reference to giving up one's religious garb (habit or cassock) and dressing as a layman.

What's "laicized"?
Laicization is the canonical process through which a priest voluntarily gives up both the rights and obligations of the priesthood. Strictly speaking, a "laicized" priest does not again become a member of the laity.

Tonsure and the "Minor" League

In the past tonsure was the rite by which a layman was made a cleric. It prepared him for receiving orders. The bishop cut the hair of the candidate in front, behind, over each ear, and on the crown of the head and invested him with a surplice (a loose, white, shirt-like garment). That "Friar Tuck look" or, in the case of some religious orders, one that was even more severe was considered a visible sign of the clerical state and was seen to symbolize Christ's crown of thorns.

Once a man was properly tonsured, the "minor" orders followed:

- Doorkeeper or porter. This order was known since the third century. Its early duties included guarding the entrance to the assembly of Christians to keep out "undesirables." Later the job evolved to ringing the bells, opening the church and sanctuary, and opening the book for the preacher.

- Lector or reader. This one has been known since the second century. At first duties included "intoning lessons and blessing bread and all first fruits." Later the role was to sing certain non-Gospel readings at Mass.

- Exorcist. In the early Church the exorcist's roles were to "cast out devils, to warn the people that noncommunicants should make room for communicants, and to pour out the water needed in divine service." At ordination the man was given the "book of exorcisms." Even prior to the post-Vatican II changes, the order's duties had become obsolete, and it was simply a step to the priesthood. The function of exorcist came to be reserved to specially delegated priests.

- Acolyte. This was the highest of the minor orders. An acolyte's duties were to serve at Mass. Even when this was an order, a layman or boy could perform all those duties and was also referred to as an acolyte.

The "major" orders were subdeacon, deacon, and priest. Subdeacon was the lowest of the three. It was first mentioned in the middle of the third century and was regarded as minor until the thirteenth. Then it was dubbed major in the West but remained minor in the East.

A subdeacon had specific duties at liturgical worship, especially at Mass. What also made his position significant was that at ordination, the candidate pledged to maintain lifelong celibacy, as well as pray the Liturgy of the Hours daily ("say the Breviary").

In 1972, Pope Paul VI abolished the orders of porter, exorcist, and subdeacon. He decreed that laity, as well as candidates for the diaconate and priesthood, can be installed (rather than "ordained") in the ministries (rather than "orders") of acolyte and lector. The pontiff confirmed the suppression of tonsure and its replacement with a service of dedication to God and to the Church. Now a man enters the "clerical state" on ordination to the diaconate. It's then that he promises to remain celibate, unless he has already done so in a religious order.

NINE

Marriage: God's Grace Through the Years

Jesus instituted the sacrament of marriage, but obviously, he didn't "invent" marriage itself. Marriage, in one form or another, has been around since the dawn of history.

Our ancestors paired up and raised families. In some cultures where polygamy was accepted, people formed more than just pairs. Yet God created one woman for Adam, and Jesus confirmed that this was God's plan from the beginning (see Mt 19:4-6).

Since then down to our own time, marriage has existed inside and outside the Church. That's even a distinction and a description that's commonly used: A couple is married "in the Church" or "outside the Church."

"Outside the Church" might mean a quick, inexpensive civil ceremony before a justice of the peace. Or it could be a wedding that takes months to plan and costs tens of thousands of dollars and at which the couple exchange vows before a nondenominational minister.

"In the Church" means the marital promises are made within the sacrament of matrimony and within the discipline of the Catholic Church.

Unlike some of the other sacraments (Eucharist, for example), there is no exact moment in the Gospels when Jesus "raised" marriage to a sacrament. (The same can be said for confirmation and anointing of the sick.) Still, through the development of doctrine (the Church, led by the Holy Spirit, coming to better understand divine revelation), it came to be understood that marriage *is* one of those seven sacraments.

It's in the story of the wedding feast at Cana—the site of Christ's first miracle (Jn 2:1-11)—that the Church sees "the confirmation of the goodness of marriage and the proclamation that thenceforth marriage will be an efficacious sign of Christ's presence." Jesus was at Cana, and through this sacrament he can be present in a couple's marriage today. Very simply put, he's on the guest list every time the sacrament is celebrated. He never fails to attend, and he never fails to bring the perfect gift: the Holy Spirit.

Christ, His Church, and His Cross

And at that wedding, in that marriage, the bride and groom say something about Christ without ever needing to say a word. Paul was speaking to married couples when he wrote to the Christians in Ephesus: "Husbands, love your wives just as Christ loved the church and gave himself up for her" (Eph 5:25). And a little later: "'For this reason a man will leave his father and mother and be joined to his wife, and the two will become one flesh.' This is a great mystery, and I am applying it to Christ and the church" (vv. 31-32).

Christ loves the Church as a groom loves his bride. In part, that's why even though a lot of people think that the sacrament of marriage is individualistic—that it belongs to the couple exchanging vows—it's much, much more. Like all the sacraments, it belongs to the Church, and it's always a communal celebration, not a private ceremony (even when the official guest list is short).

Amid the wide grins and the tears of joy, the real key to the sacrament of marriage is death. Not the "till death do us part" section of the vows but the Paschal mystery. It's by following Christ, renouncing themselves, and taking up their crosses that a husband and wife will be able to receive the original meaning of marriage and live it with the help of Christ. This grace of Christian marriage is "a fruit of Christ's cross, the source of all Christian life" (CCC 1615; see Mt 19:11).

The Paschal mystery: The cross leads to death, which leads to life.

Fundamentally, in a marriage two people believe that God is calling them to be an instrument of his love for the other person. In that mutual "act of death"—I die for you, you die for me—life comes. That's so even within sexuality. Sex isn't supposed to be about self-fulfillment but about trying to fulfill the other. And it's in trying to fulfill the other that the whole notion of God's bringing life through family, through children, comes.

Defining the Sacrament

What makes the sacrament of marriage a sacrament? What sets it apart from the civil ceremony or the nondenominational wedding?

First, for a marriage to be a sacrament for a baptized Catholic, it has to take place in the Church and be blessed by the Church. So anytime a Catholic enters a marriage that takes place under any other circumstance, the Church doesn't regard that marriage as a sacrament. It has to be within the context of the Church and be blessed according to the laws of the Church.

This is a struggle for some people. A man or woman married outside the Church may say, "I *feel* like our marriage really is a sacrament," but a sacrament isn't about feeling. We can feel a lot of things that aren't true. Bringing home a loaf of bread and praying the words of consecration over it doesn't make it the Body of Christ, even if the person saying those words really *feels* it has become the Eucharist.

Second: Both people in the marriage need to have the intention of entering the sacrament of marriage. It's not possible to have the sacrament when one person says, "I'm going to enter this and live it," and the other person says, "I'm going to go into this and try it out, and if it doesn't work I'm going to fool around on the side." That's contrary to the sacrament. That can be the basis for an annulment, the Church's declaration that, in fact, there was no marriage. *(Go to "Q & A: On Annulments," p. 155.)*

It's not possible for only one member of that couple to receive the sacrament. Both people need to intend to have a sacrament in the Catholic Church *even if one of them isn't Catholic.*

They also both have to have the ability and the capacity to be in a sacrament. That means each person has to have some level of maturity and some level of understanding of what a sacrament is. And he or she must have the capability of sharing an intimate, common life with someone. An inability or incapacity can also be the basis for an annulment.

Third: In order for a marriage to be a sacrament, each partner really has to be open to receiving the gift of grace.

The Gift of Grace in Marriage

Since mutual giving, dying to self, and loving family life can take place in marriages outside the Church, why go through the "hassle" of getting married in the Church? Why bother jumping through the "hoops" the Church has set up? (We'll talk about those later in this chapter.)

This isn't just about a church wedding (a ceremony in a particular building) but a sacramental marriage. It's about sacramental grace on that couple's wedding day and two years, ten years, fifty years down the road.

Again (a quick review here), grace is *not*

- a thing
- measurable
- delivered in a handy two-ounce sample bottle as God's gift to the happy couple (so they better use it sparingly)

Grace *is*
- in marriage, as in all aspects of our lives, a *Person*
- in its essence, the presence of God

The word itself comes from the Latin *gratia*, which also gives us "gratis"—meaning something for free. The Church tells us that grace is the free and unmerited favor of God. A couple can't buy it. A couple can't earn it. A couple—no matter how loving and wonderful—doesn't rack up grace like a reward-points program each time they use a certain credit card.

Grace is a blessing. It is the favor of God himself.

Again, obviously, grace isn't somehow limited to the sacrament of marriage. All of salvation history is grace. But the Church also tells us that grace comes to us as a personal gift. With regard to this sacrament, grace is not just a gift from God that's offered to the Church, it's not just a gift from God that's offered to an individual, but it's also a gift from God that's offered to a married couple.

What that means is that at the heart of a marriage can be a divine indwelling: God living—dwelling—within that husband and wife because of sacramental grace. They are—through all the years—the "two or three gathered in my name," and Jesus is in their midst (Mt 18:20).

When the sacrament is celebrated—and, again, a sacrament is by definition efficacious—God's grace is there. As with baptism, confirmation, Eucharist, and the rest, *God shows up.* He is present in sacramental grace—every time, without fail, no exceptions.

But even though God shows up, in all his power and goodness, human beings must accept the gift of grace. In order for grace to really take root and bear fruit, a human being must cooperate with it. And in marriage *two* people must cooperate.

Accomplishing the Impossible

How does grace bear fruit in a marriage? The ways are unlimited because God is unlimited. When a husband and wife receive grace, they receive things like the power of God, the mercy of God, the hope of God, the possibilities of God.

Just as God is unlimited, with his grace there are unlimited possibilities. That's what Scripture is telling us when it says that for us humans some things simply aren't possible, but "for God all things are possible" (Mt 19:26). What better way to start a marriage, to live a married life, than with limitless possibilities?

With grace the couple receives the strength of God. A husband and wife receive the potential of God's healing, and not only for themselves but in such a way that each can become an instrument of God's healing for other people. They receive the ability to forgive in places where they never thought they could do that. They receive the challenge of God, calling them to new heights, enabling them to live differently than they ever thought they could live.

Through grace, with grace, a wife and a husband receive the truth of God, and while the truth will set them free, the truth can be scary (see Jn 8:32). That's one of the reasons a person might not open himself or herself to God's grace. It *does* require truth, and a lot of us avoid the truth about ourselves, about our lives, about who we are and what we've done. We can't sidestep reality if we open ourselves to God's grace, because God is truth and his light brings truth.

Those are just some of the characteristics of grace—just a few of the possibilities when an individual, when a couple, receives God's grace.

In a nutshell, acceptance of this gift means a husband or wife—a couple—isn't stuck. He can change. She can change. They can change. God's gift of grace tells them that they can be different than they are right now. They can be better.

That's one basic reason why, when a couple having marital problems comes to the parish priest and asks, "Father, should we separate?" it's hard for the priest to answer. Yes, certainly, if there's violence involved. Yes, if a spouse or a child is in danger. But in other situations the question becomes, Are you open to the grace of God? Will you cooperate with God's grace? There is hope for a marriage when each spouse opens up to God's grace and to the possibility of change.

How Grace "Works"

There's another characteristic of grace (both in and beyond marriage) that's important to note and remember. The Church teaches that grace builds on nature. What that means is that God's presence doesn't overwhelm the natural.

Yes, there are exceptions. There are miracles. But for example, if someone has cancer, the vast majority of the time God's healing is going to come through the medical steps that person takes to recover. Yes, pray for God's healing, pray for a cure, *and* go see the doctor. God's grace isn't either/or. It's both/and.

What does this mean in the sacrament of marriage? If a relationship is in trouble, a husband or wife can't simply—even if sincerely—pray, "God fix this," and then sit back and wait for changes to happen, wait for healing to occur. And because at its core this sacrament involves two people, even if one works at it, even if one is open to God's grace and responds in the best ways possible, the other may still walk out the door.

Small wonder that, sometimes, the one who has prayed and worked and changed can end up feeling betrayed by God. But God is not a warden. He never takes away free will. Marital grace is available to the couple, but each partner must choose to accept it. God isn't going to come in and overwhelm a situation unless people use their freedom to allow that to happen. (The Holy Spirit nudges, but he never shoves.)

The way that grace will typically work is with human intentions and human efforts. What grace does is provide the opportunity for the couple to go over and above their own human abilities. God's presence—grace—will take their natural human state, their natural human abilities, and help them go beyond those. A wife will be stronger than she thought she could be. A husband will be more merciful. As a couple they will be more forgiving, more honest, than they could be on their own.

But if that husband decides he's going to be a liar, grace isn't going to somehow just come on him and make him tell the truth. He has to decide he wants to be a truthful person, and in his efforts to be that, God and his grace can strengthen that man and make him more that way.

As God's grace builds on the efforts and desires of that husband and wife, it continues to take their marriage—to take them—to new levels.

The Church's Do's and Don'ts

Now a bit about those ecclesiastical "hoops"—the do's and don'ts of getting married in the Church. As every engaged couple knows or very quickly learns, typically there are countless details that go into planning a wedding, and it's not hard to confuse canon law with parish regulations. "Who can marry in the Church" can seem to be on a par with "Six months' notice needed" and "No throwing rice on the front steps." Adding to that potential for misunderstanding, it's the parish that sees to it that universal Church law, diocesan regulations, and facility housekeeping rules are followed.

Let's start with the Church. Canon law says a baptized man and woman who are free to contract marriage and who freely express their consent can receive this sacrament. That "double" freedom is critical. It means neither person is under any constraint and neither is impeded by any natural or ecclesiastical law.

The exchange of consent between the spouses is the indispensable element that makes the marriage. If consent is lacking, there is no marriage. Consent means the human act by which the partners mutually give themselves to each other. "I take you to be my wife"; "I take you to be my husband."

Simply saying the words isn't enough. The consent must be an act of will of each, free of coercion or grave external fear. If the freedom is lacking, the marriage is invalid.

The Church also says

- Because sacramental marriage is a liturgical act, it's appropriate that it should be celebrated in the public liturgy of the Church.
- Marriage introduces one into an ecclesial order (we talked about that at the beginning of chapter eight) and creates rights and duties in the Church between the spouses and toward children.

- Since marriage is a state of life in the Church, certainty about it is necessary. That's why witnesses are mandatory.
- The public character of the consent protects the "I do" once given and helps the spouses remain faithful. They take their vows in front of God, his Church, and his people.

Getting Ready to Live the Sacrament

From the Church's point of view, getting to the "I do" means focusing on the sacrament of marriage, not, for example, the color of the bridesmaids' dresses. The Church says that preparation for marriage is of prime importance.

About-to-be newlyweds can learn a great deal about the sacrament of marriage from those who are living it. The *Catechism* points out that the teaching and the example given by parents and families remain the special form of preparation. Then, too, pastors and others in the Christian community (the "family of God") play a key role in handing on both the human and Christian values of marriage and family. That's true "much more so in our era when many young people experience broken homes which no longer sufficiently assure this situation" (CCC 1632).

Then, too, particular concern is shown for both "mixed marriages" (a Catholic and a non-Catholic Christian) and those in which there is a "disparity of cult" (a Catholic and a non-baptized person). *(Go to "Mixed Marriage: Handle With Care,"* p. 157.)

Typically it's the diocese that determines the formal program for all couples in all its parishes. For example, it's the diocese that says that couples, in order to properly prepare for the marriage (not just get ready for the wedding), need to begin the process at least four, five, or six months before the wedding date. It's the diocese that determines what form of religious education about the sacrament and about marriage itself is necessary. It's the diocese that declares, "These are the regulations, and here are the reasons for them" so don't go 'shopping around' parish to parish trying to find a shortcut."

Again, typically there are also regulations about active parish membership in order to be married at a particular parish. Not because "Father wants to be sure you're using your envelopes," but so a couple doesn't ask for marriage in the Church simply to please Mom and Dad or simply because the bride has always dreamed of a big church wedding. Neither should a couple be choosing to be married in a particular parish because they really like the look of the church building or because it's located close to the hall they've booked for their reception.

To ask to be married in the Church means to ask for, and agree to live, the sacrament of marriage.

Although in our society it's common for a couple to live together before marriage, it's inappropriate for those who are committed to the gospel and seeking to have a Christian marriage.

The Sacrament That's "Mutually Conferred"

Again, as with the other sacraments, the rite for marriage is simple. In the Latin tradition the bride and groom, as ministers of Christ's grace, mutually confer on each other the sacrament of matrimony by expressing their consent before the Church. A priest or deacon who assists at the celebration receives the consent of the spouses in the name of the Church and gives the blessing of the Church. His presence—and the presence of witnesses—visibly expresses the fact that marriage is an ecclesial reality.

The liturgy—even within the framework of the Mass—includes a number of prayers of blessings and an epiclesis (the calling down of the Holy Spirit) asking for grace and blessing on the new couple, especially the bride. In the epiclesis the spouses receive the Holy Spirit as the communion of love of Christ and the Church. The Holy Spirit is the seal of their covenant and the ever-available source of their love. On their wedding day and on all the days that follow, he offers them the strength to renew the fidelity they have pledged.

Q & A: On Annulments

What's the difference between an annulment and a divorce?
A divorce is an action in civil court that dissolves a marriage. An annulment is a declaration by an ecclesial court that there never was a marriage.

On what grounds would the Church declare that?

Broadly speaking, the man or woman wasn't free to contract marriage because of being under constraint or impeded by a natural or ecclesiastical law. Examples could be a young woman who feels she must marry because she sees no other way of getting out of an abusive home life. Or a man could be impeded because retardation or illness has denied him the mental capacity to make a mature decision. Another impediment is that of the man or woman already being married.

The Code of Canon Law, the book of the Church's laws, includes a number of objective factors, including fear and impediments, but subjective intentions are also considered. If, very simply put, either party said "Yes" to all that marriage involves but mentally had his or her "fingers crossed," the marriage could be invalid. Similar is the case when excluded from that consent was some essential element of marriage—for example, the permanence of the bond ("If I get tired of him, I'm going to dump him"); or the openness to children ("She may want kids, but there's no way I will ever let that happen").

Another factor could be purposeful deceit: not telling a fiancé something that's important to married life. An example would be not disclosing a medical condition that makes having children impossible.

What "ecclesial court" makes the decision?

A Church tribunal. Again, typically the process would begin in the parish and then be handled by the diocese.

Mixed Marriage: Handle With Care

When the Church talks about a "mixed marriage," it means a marriage between a Catholic and a baptized non-Catholic. It uses the term "marriage with a disparity of cult" to refer to one between a Catholic and a non-baptized person.

In the first instance the Church advises a pastor and a couple to pay particular attention. In the second it notes that "even greater circumspection" is required.

The Church says that in a successful mixed marriage the husband and wife place in common what they have received from their respective communities, and they learn from each other the way in which each lives in fidelity to Christ. Even so, it cautions, the difficulties of mixed marriages mustn't be underestimated.

A disparity of cult can present even greater difficulties. Tragically, differences about faith and the very notion of marriage and different religious mentalities can become sources of tension. That can be especially so as regards the education of children. The temptation to religious indifference, a truce in which no religion is lived, can result. Thus the Church requires an express dispensation from this impediment in order for the marriage to be valid.

TEN

How You Can Better Appreciate and Celebrate the Sacraments

Yes, being efficacious (and you know what that means), the sacraments always "work," but they can "work better" in you. They can "work better" in your family and your faith community.

What does that mean? A limited analogy (and a silly one, which makes it easy to remember) is that of a car that's properly maintained and sensibly driven. It's going to get more miles per gallon than one that needs a tune-up, has low tire pressure, and so on.

Of course, there is no measure of grace-per-reception when it comes to the celebration of a sacrament. The presence of God within you can't be quantified because infinite is infinite. But these seven gifts can "work better" within you (your family and your faith community) in the sense of your being more open to the grace being given, better recognizing that Infinite Love by expanding your own limited view of love, better appreciating what has taken place—what always takes place when a sacrament is celebrated—and, in turn, better using that love, that presence, your God, in all aspects of your life.

Another incomplete (and silly) analogy: The Holy Spirit wants to be that bright red sock in the load of white laundry that is your life. Everything is touched, tinged, turned pink.

There are ways to make your wash "pinker."

Here are ten suggestions for you, your family, and your parish:

1. Remember that the sacraments are communal in nature.

For you: One basic way to better appreciate and celebrate the sacraments as an individual is to remember that your relationship with God is not individualistic. "Just Jesus and me" is not a Catholic concept. Based on our Jewish heritage—we owe so much to our elder brothers and sisters in the faith—we see we're always part of the "we," part of the "tribe." Even when we sing a song or recite a psalm that says "I," it's in the context of "we," in the context of the Church, in the context of the people of God.

It may be necessary for you to adjust your thinking about the sacraments and, with that, to always make an effort when you celebrate a sacrament to include other people.

For your family: Instead of trying to exclude people or limit the number of people—at a baptism or wedding, for example—your family can choose to include more people. Certainly, the family budget may mean that to do this you'll host a simpler reception.

For your faith community: The parish can make available opportunities for communal anointing of the sick and reconciliation. Parish leaders can keep talking about, and preaching on, the importance of being part of a community.

2. Take the time to plan better liturgies.

For you: Prepare to celebrate a sacrament. (You might, for example, read the Sunday Gospel at home before heading for Mass.) Take an active role at the liturgy: pray, listen, respond, sing.

For your family: Celebrate the sacraments together. Go to the same Sunday Mass. Attend a communal reconciliation service. Get siblings involved in the preparations for a member's baptism or confirmation. For a wedding, don't let the planning of the sacrament take a back seat to the details of the reception.

Your faith community: At times it may feel like an uphill battle, but continue to invite, encourage, and welcome new members to take part in the variety of volunteer opportunities that go into making dynamic parish liturgies. Choose good music. Encourage those in attendance to participate. Work hard at hospitality so all feel welcome.

3. Pray before celebrating a sacrament, to better experience Christ in it rather than just "going through" the ceremony.

As an individual, family, and parish, ask the Holy Spirit to prepare you for what is about to happen. Say a prayer for others who will be taking part.

4. Receive the sacraments more frequently, especially reconciliation and Holy Communion.

For you: Go to reconciliation! Don't let fear or embarrassment stop you from hearing those comforting words: "I absolve you ..."

Attend a weekday Mass. Make the effort to get to that early celebration, or find a noontime Mass you can scoot over to during your lunch hour.

For your family: Months ahead, include in the family's schedule a weekday Mass to mark the anniversary of a wedding or of the death of a loved one. Also, pencil in "reconciliation" occasionally, and extend the celebration to dinner out or a stop for ice cream afterwards.

For your faith community: Make those weekday opportunities available: an "early-riser" liturgy; a noon celebration or evening Mass once a week; reconciliation in the late afternoon—as a "quick stop" between work and home or as a prelude to an evening Mass.

Give parishioners what they want (which is, of course, also what they need, because it's what all of us need: God's grace). And keep in mind their time constraints as you get the word out: "The early Mass will begin at 7:00, and you can be on the road heading for work by 7:30. Guaranteed." This doesn't mean a "drive-through" approach or attitude but the liturgy properly adapted to serve the community.

5. Continue your education on the sacraments.

For you: Read the *Catechism of the Catholic Church.* It's a fantastic book and a rich resource. Attend a class. Check out what's available online. Subscribe to a Catholic periodical. Read a book. Become an RCIA or OCI sponsor.

For your family: Leave those books and periodicals out around the house. Encourage your children—your godchildren, your nieces and nephews, your grandchildren—to ask questions about spirituality and the Church. (Teens tend to have no problem in this area.) If you're unsure what the Church teaches or why it teaches that, find out with your child.

For your faith community: Make those classes available, or let parishioners know about neighboring parishes or local Catholic colleges hosting classes. Use the weekly bulletin for catechesis, but remember your audience. Consider not just what you want to share with them but *how* you want to share it.

It might be a very simple flier on how to go to confession. The same material could be available in the church by the reconciliation room. ("Bring this in with you if it helps! It's not cheating!")

Let your community members know if you spot a good Web site. Invite them to be sacramental sponsors by clearly spelling out what's expected of someone in that role. Know the most common concerns or objections ("I think it will take too much time." "I don't know enough." "I'm not holy enough.") and address those.

You're like a good waiter—you *are* a servant, after all—who knows what's in the kitchen and is happy to make recommendations. These days (as always), there's a tremendous hunger for spirituality.

6. Keep the focus on the primary symbols of each sacrament.

As an individual, family, and parish, remember and recognize the symbols that are used and accept no substitutes. Butterflies, rainbows, "unity candles" at weddings, and all the rest may be popular, and they may truly have value, but they aren't the symbols of the sacraments.

The symbols of the sacraments *are* very basic (and the ceremonies *are* very simple). They may, at times, seem to lack the razzle-dazzle needed to "sell" something today. But the Church isn't selling; Christ is freely giving. Those very basic symbols—bread, water, oil, and the rest—help focus attention on a very basic message: God loves you and wants to fill you with grace. They help focus attention on the very basic—and amazing!—reality of what takes place during the celebration of a sacrament.

Certainly one way a parish can highlight a symbol is by displaying the oils in church. Giving them a prominent and proper place not only illustrates respect for the symbol and the sacraments but encourages learning. "Hey, what's the deal with that stuff in the bottles?"

7. Get involved in the parish liturgy committee.

For you: There's a place for your talents. Many parts, and many volunteers, go into making a good celebration. This not only helps others better understand the sacraments but also keeps your knowledge and creativity fresh.

For your family: Keep an eye out for how your family can take part and for ways you can—gently!—suggest volunteering. Maybe you can all help with the pre-Easter church cleaning or can bring up the gifts during Mass. When a child reaches the age to become an altar server, you could encourage that.

For your faith community: A parish needs to provide a variety of opportunities and consider how best to use the gifts of its many talented community members. People want good liturgies!

At times that may mean not simply bemoaning a lack of "new blood" but truly welcoming others who have new suggestions. It's no secret that parish committees, made up of human beings, can become stagnant and territorial. Sometimes key leaders or "worker bees" burn out but remain in office because no one seems to be stepping forward to take up the mantle.

On the flip side, those who would like to volunteer hesitate because those now serving have done it for so long and know so much. The rookie with an idea might be told, "We tried that. It didn't work." True. In 1985.

It's good to keep in mind that just as the Holy Spirit blew through the Upper Room, he may well blow through a parish committee and rattle the rafters a bit.

8. Enrich your celebration of the sacraments by incorporating other prayer forms in your life.

For you: Remember that the sacraments aren't the only Catholic form of prayer. Read Scripture. Spend time before the Blessed Sacrament. Say the rosary or pray the stations of the cross. Again, take advantage of the Church's heritage, the rich variety of prayer that is available. It may be that at a particular time in your life one form has a special appeal. Reconsider one that in the past didn't "grab you"; now it may bring great comfort.

For your family: All those practices can also be done as a family. Part of parents' (godparents', grandparents', aunts', and uncles') responsibilities to younger family members can be introducing that prayer heritage.

For your faith community: In the same way, a parish can provide and promote opportunities—adoration of the Blessed Sacrament or a Holy Hour, for example. Then, too, basic education about various prayer forms can be included in the bulletin, on fliers, on a parish Web site: "How to Say the Rosary," "Favorite Morning and Evening Prayers," "Bible-Reading Basics," "Praying the Liturgy of the Hours," and so on.

Most often this doesn't mean parish staff or volunteers need to develop a lot of teaching materials. Rather it's a matter of finding and taking advantage of solid material that has already been written and is in the public domain—that is, its use is not limited by a copyright.

9. Have family activities that will draw the family closer to the sacraments.

You, your family, and your faith community can plan and celebrate activities and occasions that are "sacramental." At home it can be eating dinner together, having a "family night," or volunteering together on a service project. At the parish there can be communal celebrations outside the sacraments. The annual dinners, the "spring fling" or "fall fest" weekends, the parish picnic or campout, and all the rest can help build community and help each member feel he or she is a part of something bigger. Each is.

10. Use Christian symbols.

While it's important to maintain the sacraments' symbols, there are other symbols—and sacramentals—that you, your family, and your faith community can use outside the sacraments. Each is designed to help make a person (a family, a parish) more aware of the presence of Christ in daily life. Examples would be displaying a crucifix, an image (a statue; an icon; a painting of Christ, Mary, or a saint), or a symbol of the faith; having a Bible out (not just "for show" but for handy use); and listening to Christian and liturgical music.

More than only reminders for ourselves, symbols can say to others, "I am a Catholic; my family is Catholic; my parish is Catholic."

But What If ...?

Maybe you're not Catholic. Or maybe you're Catholic but unable to receive the sacraments. There are still ways you and your family can participate in a faith community and can better appreciate the sacraments.

We humans are limited in so many ways. And while the sacraments are seven specific outward signs Christ chose and began in order to give us grace, our infinite, all-loving God is certainly not limited to them.

And learning more about the sacraments can in itself be an effective means of grace. You can come to know and recognize Christ's presence in them, and you can be part of their celebration.

If You're a Catholic Who Can't Receive the Sacraments

If you married outside the Church, either because of a previous marriage or simply by choice, you're missing something, but you're still very much a part of the family. We long to share the sacraments with you, and so we encourage you to keep honoring the sacraments:

- Come to Mass. You may want to ask the priest if you can come forward for a blessing at Communion time.
- Seek out ways you can be appropriately involved in the ministries of the Church.
- Take the time to meet with a priest or parish staff member to find out what can be done to bring you into full communion with the Church. If the "external forum solution" cannot rectify the situation, you may wish to discuss with your confessor the possibility of the "internal forum solution." It would allow you, under special circumstances, to receive the sacraments.

A forum is a place of judgment. In the Church, there are two forums. One is the external forum. This has to do with public settings, public records, and jurisdiction used for the public good (such as a marriage tribunal).

The other forum is the internal forum. It's used in the sacrament of reconciliation. It's here that a confessor, along with the individual, judge what is best for the person's salvation and spiritual life. A confessor has some flexibility to allow a person to receive the sacraments, under certain conditions, even though the person may not be able to fulfill the requirements of the external forum.

This is consistent with the Church's pastoral concern that ultimately the good of souls is its priority.

- Encourage others to appreciate the gift of the sacraments and to continue to reverence the sacraments.
- Make special efforts to attend adoration or visit the Blessed Sacrament in order to keep a spiritual communion with Christ and the Church.

If You're a Catholic Who's Been Away From the Church for a Time

- Ask yourself why.
- Meet with a priest.
- Attend a program for returning or "re-membering" Catholics.
- Start the process of forgiving someone within the Church who has hurt you.
- Start the process of forgiving yourself.
- Remember, Christ prayed that we all would be one (in the Gospel of John), and it's the desire of Christ and of the Church to share the Eucharist and the other sacraments with you.
- No matter why you left, come home!

If You're Not a Catholic

We invite you:

- Check out the process in a parish for receiving newcomers into the Catholic Church: the Rite of Christian Initiation for Adults/Order of Christian Initiation (RCIA/OCI).
- Read one of the many good books that are available about basic Catholic teaching.
- Help Catholic family members and friends deepen their own appreciation of the presence of Christ in the sacraments as you do the same.
- Truly open your heart to the possibility of entering the Church and sharing in the grace of the sacraments.

Congratulations!

Good for you! You've looked through a book on the sacraments.

The Catholic Church has a vast catechetical richness that is thousands of years old. It's up to each generation, and each individual, to rediscover it and to explore it in order to better benefit from it personally. It's up to each generation, and each individual, not only to apply this richness to the current era and circumstances but to, in some degree, contribute to it.

We never stop being students; at times we each serve as a teacher. In either role, increasing our knowledge increases our ability to appreciate the seven gifts we call sacraments.

Those seven mysteries are God's plan for his Church and for all people. They're his plan for you.

We'll end this book by repeating what we said in the first chapter: The sacraments remain an incredible opportunity, a source of divine assistance that's unique because they were begun by Christ and delivered by the Holy Spirit. They're one-of-a-kind—because they're efficacious.

They give what they promise. Always. And what they promise is beyond description, beyond superlatives, beyond anything we can ask or imagine. The sacraments allow us to share a sliver of—get a taste of, catch a glimmer of—what is to come, or more accurately, what can come for each of us because Jesus came for each of us.

Just as we have the opportunity to "choose" heaven because we have free will, we have the privilege, time and again, to experience that sliver, that taste, that glimmer here on earth. This is all because of Christ's redemption.

More than gifts from God, the sacraments are gifts *of* God, the gift of himself to us.